D1488660

GRANT'S VICTORY

How Ulysses S. Grant Won the Civil War

Bruce L. Brager

STACKPOLE
BOOKS

Guilford, Connecticut

Published by Stackpole Books
An imprint of The Rowman & Littlefield Publishing Group, Inc.
4501 Forbes Boulevard, Suite 200, Lanham, Maryland 20706
www.rowman.com

Distributed by NATIONAL BOOK NETWORK
800-462-6420

British Library Cataloguing in Publication Information Available

Library of Congress Cataloging-in-Publication Data

Names: Brager, Bruce L., 1949- author.
Title: Grant's victory : how Ulysses S. Grant won the Civil War / Bruce L. Brager.
Description: Lanham : Stackpole Books, 2020. | Includes bibliographical references
    and index. | Summary: "Two of the great themes of the Civil War are how Lincoln
    found his war-winning general in Ulysses Grant and how Grant finally defeated
    Lee. Grant's Victory intertwines these two threads in a grand narrative that shows
    how Grant made the difference in the war. At Eastern theater battlefields from
    Bull Run to Gettysburg, Union commanders-whom Lincoln replaced after virtually
    every major battle-had struggled to best Lee, either suffering embarrassing defeat
    or failing to follow up success. Meanwhile, in the West, Grant had been refining
    his art of war at places like Fort Donelson, Shiloh, Vicksburg, and Chattanooga,
    and in early 1864, Lincoln made him general-in-chief. Arriving in the East almost
    deus ex machina, and immediately recognizing what his predecessors never could,
    Grant pressed Lee in nearly continuous battle for the next eleven months-a series
    of battles and sieges that ended at Appomattox"—Provided by publisher.
Identifiers: LCCN 2019045631 (print) | LCCN 2019045632 (ebook) | ISBN
    9780811739191 (cloth) | ISBN 9780811769112 (epub)
Subjects: LCSH: Grant, Ulysses S. (Ulysses Simpson), 1822–1885—Military
    leadership. | United States—History—Civil War, 1861–1865—Campaigns. |
    Command of troops—History—19th century. | Strategy—History—19th century. |
    United States. Army—Biography. | Generals—United States—Biography.
Classification: LCC E470 .B795 2020 (print) | LCC E470 (ebook) | DDC 973.7/3092-
    -dc23
LC record available at https://lccn.loc.gov/2019045631
LC ebook record available at https://lccn.loc.gov/2019045632

Writers read before they write.
I want to dedicate this book to the
early historians and writers who "turned me on"
to the American Civil War:

Bruce Catton
McKinley Kantor
Philip van Doren Stern
Robert Stackpole

It is impossible to conceive a field worse adapted to the movements of a grand army. . . . The whole face of the country is thickly wooded, with only an occasional opening, and intersected by a few narrow wood-roads. It was a region of gloom and the shadow of death.

—Reverend Theodore Irving, 1873[1]

CONTENTS

ACKNOWLEDGMENTS

Thank you to all the following:

The historians and writers cited in the dedication and the bibliography.

The staff at the libraries and depositaries visited during research. In particular the National Archives, the Library of Congress, the Texas State Library and Archives, public libraries for Arlington County and New York City, and the George Washington University Library.

The National Park Service facilities at Fredericksburg, Chancellorsville, and Gettysburg.

The editorial staff at Stackpole Press, including Dave Reisch, Stephanie Otto, and Elaine McGarraugh.

And anyone else I might have neglected here.

INTRODUCTION

Lost in the Woods

War has always been the province of confusion.

—Eric Durschmied, 1998[1]

Turning points, tipping points, forks in the road, contingencies, and de-cisive moments—these are all ways of describing times when history can take different paths. Tipping points tend not to splash themselves into the headlines. The points, or at least where they took place, can pass unnoticed unless one is looking for them.

One has to look carefully, to avoid having a cab driver make a wrong turn and the passenger not notice that they have just zoomed past the key historic crossroads the passenger wanted to visit. But one goes to a historic site to get a feel for what happened as well as to see where it happened. A lot of people, a lot of armies, have gotten lost, in all meanings of that word.

The crossroads in Northern Virginia, about halfway between Washing-ton, D.C., and Richmond, Virginia, is not impressive. The Orange Plank Road, Route 621, heads roughly northeast-southwest. The Brock Road, Route 613, intersects as it heads northwest-southeast. Both roads lead to Route 3, the Plank Road, the main east-west road in the area, a mile or two to the north. All three roads existed at the time of the American Civil War, when this area became famous as the site of four of the bloodiest battles in which the United States ever took part.

Fredericksburg, the site of the December 1862 battle, is about ten miles to the east of the crossroads in question. The Plank Road, Route 3, will take you into town, past the site of the Chancellorsville campaign engagement at Salem Church, and past Spotsylvania Mall, the site of one of the 2002 Washington, D.C., sniper killings.

Spotsylvania, the site of the May 1864 battle that took place about a week after the Battle of the Wilderness, is about eight miles to the southeast, along the Brock Road. The sites of the May 1863 Battle of Chancellorsville and the May 1864 Battle of the Wilderness partly intersect, though not all the area is preserved by the National Park Service. Housing and related development are encroaching in the area. Orange Plank Road, outside of National Park Service land, has been widened and improved in the last few years, clearly to make room for new housing, and, perhaps appropriately, a new cemetery. The good thing is that at least two of the developments are set back and not visible from the roads. The effect is far more attractive, and far less confused, than some housing developments closer to Fredericksburg.

Historic preservationists have different motives. Preserved historic areas exist for different reasons. They can mark significant events, such as those in the Fredericksburg area. They can honor the lives of great Americans, such as George Washington's home at Mount Vernon. They can preserve at least a little of the feel of past periods, such as historic downtown Fredericksburg.

One visits these areas for different reasons. One reason is that one gets dragged by family. Such was the boy at Antietam I once heard asking his father, "Who won here, the British or the Americans?" One can go to study the ground, or to gain specific knowledge about the events, or almost just to meditate and think about what happened. One can even learn accidentally, and not always the message people want to teach.

For one quick example, fast food places near historic sites do not teach the desired lessons of the preservationists. But they do show the end result of history, the establishment of a consumer society. And they avoid the excess formality, the coldness, for which other countries have become notorious. Fortunately the only fast food places near the Fredericksburg area parks, though just about every inch of the area played a role in the battles, are near Salem Church, the site of a part of the Battle of Chancellorsville disconnected from the main fighting.

My own recent trip to Fredericksburg was part of the research for this book. I learned lessons, from myself as well as from others, though not always the ones I planned to learn. Planning was the first lesson; overall planning and how one carries out the plans. First of all, how do you dress when it is 48 degrees at 7 a.m., when one leaves for an early train—I don't own a car—and going up to 80 degrees later that day? Wear a light sweater under one's jacket seemed like a good idea. Probably was, though the sweater had to be carried most of the day.

The second lesson is how to pack. I use a light travel bag as a camera case. This may be mislearning from a few years ago, when a camera in a camera case got left in a New York City cab. A small case had made the camera less conspicuous, and I gave more attention to my laptop computer. I lost a Nikon, of course, as what is the fun in losing a cheap camera. My sister asked me if my name was on the camera. I said that next time I do something stupid I will plan better.

When I went to Fredericksburg I should have taken time to see if the camera would fit into the briefcase I was also carrying, or carried it in the open. The new jacket I wore had a lot of pockets, and might have been put to better use. Two cases got awfully heavy as the day wore on. During the Civil War, new recruits carried a lot of stuff with them when they went on campaign marches. They quickly learned to leave in camp, or even just dump, what was not absolutely necessary. One travels to historic sites to learn about history. Another lesson of history is the need to start out with a well-considered plan. A related lesson is that plans fall apart.

Plans started to fall apart with Amtrak, our national passenger railroad. The train, due at Fredericksburg at 8:35, after a forty-eight-minute ride, arrived at 9:25, more late than the planned duration of the ride itself. This, it should be noted, was a day before the entire northeast corridor train service went down due to an electrical blackout.

The town visitors' center gave me the name of a cab company to get me out to the Chancellorsville area about ten miles west of town. I did not think to ask if the drivers were competent and knew where they were going.

Making my way by foot to the National Park Service Visitors' Center, I saw that the Sunken Road, the center of the December 1862 Battle of Fredericksburg, has been closed off to traffic and restored to a more parklike appearance, giving it a period feel—at least until the backhoe, or whatever it was, drove by.

I had to take a cab—I don't have a car and am a VERY inexpert driver—to the Tapp Farm, about a mile down the Orange Plank Road, from the central crossroads. The Tapp Farm is a very interesting place, a place where, in two separate incidents, Robert E. Lee ran the serious risk of capture or death.

Even with a map, the cab driver got me a couple of miles down Brock Road. I recall thinking on the drive that I have to check out some Park Service signs on the right of the Orange Plank Road. The signs had not moved;

I did not notice when the cab driver turned down the wrong road. The historic lesson here is not just, "If I hire an idiot, what does that make me for hiring an idiot?" but the need not just to create a plan and give appropriate orders, but to monitor implementation. Plans do not carry themselves out.

However, my immediate problem seemed a workable one to solve. After arranging to be picked up at the Chancellorsville center several miles away, not trusting my new cell phone, I decided to head through a patch of woods instead of around them. These woods played a part in both battles. Confederate maneuvers here in 1864 almost cost the North the battle. Lieutenant General Thomas J. "Stonewall" Jackson marched through here in 1863, with his entire corps, on the way to his smashingly effective flank attack.

Amazing how long it can take to walk through what seemed like a small woods. Boots get badly scratched in such woods; fortunately, the boots were very old. Cell phone becomes a dead weight, shoving me back to 1864 communications. But soon the sun gets far enough to the west to be useful for rough direction finding. A several-millennium-old system of navigation worked.

Awesome to think what it must have been like in similar woods, though worse, blinded by smoke, trying to walk as quietly as possible to avoid alerting your enemy, or having bullets come out of the mist from an enemy you could not see. This must have been terrifying, and it increases my respect for those who functioned in it, whatever uniform they wore. I tried a few steps with my eyes closed. That was bad enough.

The soldiers marching through the woods, sometimes getting as lost as I seemed to be, were the boots on the ground—we will likely always need boots on the ground, though with current technology, hopefully working better than my cell phone—who had to carry out the best-laid plans of their generals. And I knew that I would eventually reach the Brock or the Orange Plank Road and be able to get oriented. When the soldiers reached a clearing they would be far better targets for the enemy. And if they were wounded, and not quickly rescued, they faced a worse fate when the heavy brush on the ground caught fire. The lucky wounded, of those left on the field, were killed by the smoke, or rendered unconscious, before the flames reached them and either burned them to death or ended their lives by exploding the gunpowder in their pouches.

At one point I heard a variation on the crunching of the brush—a metallic clink. Unfortunately, the shovel I stepped on was far too new to be worth recovering. I also don't think the rusty beer can I saw was Confederate issue.

About the time the sun had moved far enough to the west for me to use it for navigation, I noticed the first of many large toppled trees, seemingly ripped out by the roots. A couple of weeks before my trip there had been heavy thunderstorms, and a possible tornado, in the area. Later on a Park Service ranger said the trees were probably destroyed by Hurricane Isabelle, three years before my walk. Remind me not to hike a battlefield during a hurricane, or a thunderstorm, or a heavy late June rain for that matter. Armed men are not the only thing that can damage or destroy a forest.

There is some consolation that the housing developers in the area seem to have at least some concern for scenic easements, minimizing the visual impact of their developments on the area. Interesting to find out, though, where the residents work—Fredericksburg is part of the Washington, D.C., metropolitan area. Commutes get longer and longer. There were a lot of people getting off the commuter rail trains that evening at the train station.

About two hours after I began my walk in the woods, I finally made it to the crossroads in question. And my cell phone finally got reception.

1

AN ORDINARY CROSSROADS

We rely greatly on the sure operation of a complete blockade of the Atlantic and Gulf ports soon to commence. In connection with such blockade we propose a powerful movement down the Mississippi to the ocean, with a cordon of posts at proper points . . . so as to envelop the insurgent States and bring them to terms with less bloodshed than by any other plan.

—General in Chief Winfield Scott, US Army, May 1861[1]

The decisive moment, the tipping point that presents the lesson of this story, occurred in a quite undramatic locale, an ordinary crossroads in rural Virginia, ten miles from Fredericksburg, roughly the midpoint between Washington and Richmond, the contending capitals during the American Civil War. One road in this crossroads leads to the Rappahannock River, a few miles to the north, and back to Federal fortifications in Washington, D.C. (A second branch of the crossroads leads to Richmond, Virginia.) The line of this river, and the Rapidan River, formed a "Dare Mark,"[2] the unofficial and static front for most of the Civil War in the East. Moving across this line, this trip wire by one side always provoked action by the other. Both sides also worked to draw the other away from this line.

The only visible hints of this crossroads' importance are several National Park Service signs. The passerby will learn that the crossroads are historic by some signs that say, "This is historic" and tell the reader why. The passerby will also learn that this crossroads, though the scene of heavy fighting in May 1864, is important because of another passerby, and the direction in which he chose to travel.

This crossroads, however, is where this story ends. Like most decisive moments, its importance lies in the context of its story, in what came before and in what followed. One can argue that this crossroads is where the North, figuratively, and literally, put itself on the road to victory in the American Civil War. One can argue that this insignificant location from the present is the focal point of lessons for the present from the past, lessons not just for the military but for all human endeavors. Such lessons are knowing and appreciating context, being ready to properly react to surprises as well as to expected events and developments, opportunities, and dangers within a battle, the part of a battle within a campaign, of a campaign within a war, and the need for persistence, coordination, and maximum effective use of all resources.

This story presents lessons in making decisions. Decisions in wartime, and for that matter decisions in peacetime, have kept much of their basic nature. Know the problem as it stands, be able to make a reasonable guess (you will never be certain) about how the problem will change without and with action, remember that even observation alters the reality being observed, know the resources available to you and your adversary, choose your action, monitor the results of action, and be prepared to start the whole process all over again. Remember that the true version of an old cliché should actually be, "If I knew then what I know now, and what I should have known then." Remember also, that though plans are the starting point, they are rarely the ending point. An old Russian proverb states, "The plan was smooth on paper, only they forgot about the ravines."[3]

The immediate story—the background and context began a lot earlier— begins at the end of April 1863, a few miles to the east of the crossroads. In late April 1863, when Major General Joseph Hooker led the main Federal army in the East, the Army of the Potomac, into the tangled Virginia forest known as "The Wilderness," the Civil War had been raging for two years, in the East focused on the Dare Mark. On the surface, the war should have been a quick, one-sided contest. A relatively large, rich, industrial nation was fighting a small, poor, agricultural nation. Long before Hooker took his army out of their camps north of Fredericksburg and moved them into the Wilderness, the North should have defeated the South, but had failed to do so.

The North, however, had the far harder road to victory of the two sides. The North had to actively win the war, actively conquer the South. As historian Bell I. Wiley writes,

The North unquestionably had an immense superiority of material and human resources. But the North faced a greater task. In order to win the war, the North had to subdue a vast country of nine million inhabitants, while the South would prevail by maintaining a successful resistance. To put it another way, the North had to conquer the South while the South could win by outlasting its adversary, by convincing the North that coercion was impossible or not worth the effort.[4]

As a rule—though there are exceptions to all generalizations about people—the closed South, with an economy based on slavery, distrusted, and even feared, outsiders. The free labor–based Northern system encouraged immigration from overseas, at a heavy rate, both in numbers and relative to population, comparable to the period 1880 to 1920 and 1980 to the present.[5] When the American Civil War began, the North had a vastly larger manpower base, with a white population roughly five times that of the South. The North also had the industrial resources that would be needed to run a modern, industrial war.

However, the North had to find, something by no means certain, the way to properly coordinate and apply, and to keep applying as long as necessary, its potentially overwhelming resources to defeat the South. The one physical advantage the South had, east of the Mississippi River where most of the war took place, was a large territory, roughly twice that of the North east of the Mississippi. The North had to cope with the Southern option of strategic withdrawal, sucking Yankee armies into the vast and hostile spaces. The North had to actively conquer.

The South had to be given no rest from attacks at any point, no chance to catch its breath, let alone to shift troops from location to location to meet Federal threats. But this needed the ability to coordinate armies and act in unison, what might be called coordination in space. This needed, in turn, the will to keep acting, keep pressing—coordination in time.

The American Civil War always was a war of attrition, as well as of strategy, where the enemy had to be worn down. Arguably, the strategic debate on both sides was over the balance between the two. The North has been described as a more patient society than the South. Sam Houston, governor of Texas in 1861, was one of the few unionist Southern leaders. In a speech early that year, he colorfully warned a Texas audience,

You may, after the sacrifice of countless millions of treasure and hundreds of thousands of precious lives, as a bare possibility, win Southern independence, if God be not against you; but I doubt it. I tell you that . . . the North is determined to preserve this Union. They are not a fiery, impulsive people as you are, for they live in colder climates. But when they begin to move in a given direction, where great interests are involved . . . they move with the steady momentum and perseverance of a mighty avalanche; and what I fear is, they will overwhelm the South with ignoble defeat.[6]

Staying the course, perseverance, was necessary for the war to be won. But Northern patience was not unlimited. Northern public opinion might not continue to pay the price of blood and treasure needed to give the Federal government time to find how to coordinate its resources, fully unify its people, and win the war. The Northern public, and the Northern government, only slowly realized that this would be a long war, that victory required "staying the course" and paying the price. Northern persistence, and Northern patience, required a realization of the basic attritional nature of the Civil War. American persistence would have to outweigh American desire for quick results.

The South just had to avoid losing long enough for the Northern population to lose patience and force its government to end the war. The South had to outlast the North—possibly just long enough for an outside power or powers to come to its assistance. This was not beyond the realm of possibility. The American revolutionaries got such outside assistance, and won their war against far greater odds in 1776 than the Confederacy faced in 1861.

Confederate leaders were aware of this history. Strategic debate among the high command and the political leadership centered around how much they should focus on just trying to keep the Confederacy alive, hoping to wear out Northern patience or convince European nations, particularly Great Britain, to intervene, or how actively they should take the offensive. In many ways this was a debate between Southern political perception, favoring waiting out the Federals, and what had become a Southern instinct to actively fight one's enemies and try to end the war quickly.

Since the North had to invade, waiting out the North would call for using the South's huge territory, following the example of the Russians fighting Napoleon. The South should have defended key points and let the North expend effort and manpower first in conquering and then in holding large expanses of territory.

This was politically impossible, and the Confederates paid a price. In the West—in this case meaning Tennessee, Georgia, Mississippi, Alabama, and, though it was technically part of the Union, Kentucky—efforts to defend every inch of Confederate territory, regardless of strategic value, had led to a series of defeats. When Hooker led his army into the Wilderness, Vicksburg, Mississippi, was already under siege. If Vicksburg fell, this would give the Federal government control of the Mississippi River and cut the Confederacy in two. Vicksburg was one point the Confederates had to defend, but they wasted resources elsewhere that might have been better used at Vicksburg.

Ironically, states' rights, the Southern justification for the existence of the Confederacy, made it harder for them to develop and implement an appropriate overall strategy. Southern states were no happier about centralized direction from Richmond than they had been with centralized direction from Washington. Both leaderships faced pressure from states. But the basic Confederate ideology, and his own political failings, made it much harder for Confederate president Jefferson Davis to overcome political problems and implement what he saw (probably accurately) as the best strategy for winning the war than it was for the far more politically skillful Abraham Lincoln. Davis was unable to use territory for time, unable to defend just militarily necessary points within the South.

Historians still debate what the South should have done, and if there was any way the South could have won. Most agree, however, that the South never fully worked out its overall strategy for possible victory.

The North, however, followed virtually the same strategy for the entire war. When the Civil War began in April 1861, the senior soldier in the US Army, Lieutenant General Winfield Scott, quickly created, or stumbled on, what became the rough outline of the eventual Federal plan for victory—the so-called Anaconda Plan. (This plan is sometimes credited to a female clerk in the War Department.) Basically this plan called for a naval blockade to cut the South off from outside assistance; capturing the Mississippi River, to cut the South in two; and sending armies to capture key points in the South. The Confederacy would be crushed to death, as the anaconda snake crushes its prey. But a "West to East" approach, rather than the "North to South" approach focusing on the East, was not politically feasible as the main Federal effort.

From almost the start of hostilities, the Federal government made clear and steady progress, though with a few bumps in the road—such as the major defeat at Chickamauga, October 1863—in the West. For most of the war, aided by the politically necessary but militarily misguided Confederate strategy, the Federals were better able to apply their manpower and resource advantages in the West. There was more room for the Federals to maneuver in the West than in the geographically far smaller East. The major rivers, flowing roughly north to south, served as invasion routes for the Federal armies. In many cases, Federal gun boats on the river could provide support to armies on nearby land. In the East, the major rivers, most famously the Potomac and the Rappahannock, flow west to east. They acted as barriers to invading armies.[7]

Political realities ensured that both sides would have to put their primary focus on the East, the one hundred miles between Washington, D.C., and Richmond, Virginia. All wars are political. In a very political civil war, political considerations dominate.

The Federal capital, Washington, D.C., had been there since 1800. Ironically, in the context of the Civil War, this was the result of a political deal between North and South. It was not until May 22, 1861, over a month after the Civil War started at Fort Sumter, that Confederate president Jefferson Davis signed a resolution to move the Confederate capital from Montgomery, Alabama, to Richmond, Virginia. The Confederate Congress would reconvene on July 20. One day later, the first major battle of the war took place just north of Manassas, Virginia.

The decision to move the capital to Richmond ensured its place as the most highly visible and prestigious Federal target and, for three years, focused the war just about halfway between the two capitals. "On to Richmond" became a Northern rallying cry, to the distress of President Lincoln, who considered the main Confederate army the primary Eastern target. Perhaps the importance of Richmond, and the Eastern theater, was just public perception, but in a political war perception could be vital. "What is perceived to be true is true."[8]

Politics and perception overcoming military realities and needs proved a constant headache for Lincoln. One of the main reasons Scott's Anaconda plan failed to initially take root, though the plan should be considered the indirect basis for Northern overall strategy throughout the war, was its focus on West to East advances. The main Eastern Federal army would have to stand on the defensive. This would not be popular. Scott himself recognized the political dangers with his plan. In May 1861 he wrote, "A word now as to the greatest obstacle in the way of this plan—the great danger now pressing upon us—the impatience of our patriotic and loyal Union friends. They will urge instant and vigorous action, regardless, I fear, of consequences."[9]

Whatever the real value of the Western theater, and the value of the arguments that more focus there would have ended the war sooner with a Northern victory, one should consider whether the "East first" advocates were right. How long would the Northern public have tolerated continued failure in the East for the sake of victory in the West? Even from a purely military point of view, the East could not be given second priority. Could first the Western war, and then the final coordination of attacks on all fronts, have been successful after a decisive disaster to the primary Federal army in the East, or to the command, control, and communications center for the Federal cause, Washington itself?

Even the most ardent "Western" advocates among military historians would have to concede that a major disaster was more likely in the East, since the best Confederate generals were in the East. The East's apparent importance gave it a real importance and made it the place where a quick victory in the Civil War might have been achieved.[10]

Federal overall strategy was virtually selected not long after the first Confederate artillery shells slammed into Fort Sumter. Coordinated and continuous attacks on the South from all directions were needed. The question was whether and how the North would implement its broad strategy. Could it mobilize its resources, and its determination, to stay the course, however long it took to win? Could Lincoln find a general willing to act? Winfield Scott turned seventy-five two months after the Confederates fired on Fort Sumter. Scott was too old to actively command a field army headed "on to Richmond." Lincoln always faced the issue of finding commanders fully willing to carry out the basic Federal plan. In the fall of 1861, Attorney General Edward Bates expressed this need when he wrote in his diary, "The public spirit is beginning to quail under the depressing influence of our prolonged inaction."[11]

Both sides underestimated each other. The North thought a quick "on to Richmond" campaign was enough to force one battle and win a quick victory. The South thought the same thing. The soft Yankees would be no problem, they thought. Not long after the April 1861 start of the war, one Texas volunteer captain told his company, "The war we are going into will be a breakfast spell and we are in an awful hurry to get to the front to have a part in whipping the Yankees. It is a fact that one Southern man can whip ten Yankees."[12] The period in which their questions would be answered was April 1863 to May 1864.

2

THE PENINSULA CAMPAIGN

The period of inaction has passed. I will now bring you face to face with the rebels, and only pray that God defend the right.

—George McClellan, March 1862[1]

General George B. McClellan won several small victories in western Virginia in mid-July 1861, helping hold this area under Federal control. Within a few months, this area would secede from the state of Virginia—to the outrage of Virginia officials and military officers with no sense of irony—and become West Virginia. (The overall commander of Confederate forces in the area, the forces that "lost West Virginia," was Robert E. Lee.)

On July 21, 1861, the Federals lost the first major battle of the war, at Bull Run, Virginia, just north of the town of Manassas. The next day, with the Federal rout still being digested in Washington, McClellan received a telegram from the Federal high command telling him to come to Washington. "Circumstances make your presence here necessary. Charge [William] Rosecrans or some other general with your present department and come hither without delay."[2]

McClellan arrived in Washington on July 26, and the next day he met with President Abraham Lincoln. Lincoln told him about his new command, the Division of the Potomac. This included the Washington, D.C., defenses and General Irwin McDowell's army, a few days after its defeat at the First Battle of Bull Run. McClellan soon renamed the army the Army of the Potomac.

According to historian Stephen W. Sears, General in Chief Winfield Scott, more than twice McClellan's age, was less than fully enthusiastic about McClellan's appointment. Scott "seems to have felt as a matter of principle that at thirty-four McClellan was too young to deserve command of any army, but in the event he raised no actual objection."[3] Sears goes on to point out that, at the time, there were no real grounds for objection. McClellan had done well in West Virginia. He was also, next to Scott, ranking general in the army.

McClellan immediately wrote his wife that he had been called on to save his country. Statements like this, particularly when considered with other McClellan statements about God having chosen him, seem arrogant—if not messianic—by modern standards. They would have presented far less of an image problem, at least at the start of McClellan's career in Washington, back then. Bruce Catton points out one thing more: "McClellan's boast was justified: the people *were* calling upon him to save the country."[4]

McClellan also got off to a "good" start in his relationship with President Lincoln, and the rest of the administration, by referring to the president, in letters to his wife, as "the original gorilla."[5] He had earlier written his wife that "I do not intend to be sacrificed."[6]

This might just have been a frustrated general sounding off in private, though it is hard to show respect in public that one does not feel. However, McClellan showed his attitude toward Lincoln, and probably toward any command supervision, on the night of November 13, 1861, about two weeks after taking over from General Scott, whom he had tried to undermine until Lincoln stopped his efforts. When Scott resigned, for age (seventy-five) and infirmity, McClellan was made his replacement, while keeping command of the Army of the Potomac.

On November 13, Lincoln went to visit McClellan, with Secretary of State William Seward and John Hay, one of Lincoln's two chief assistants. They were told McClellan was away, at a wedding, and decided to wait. When McClellan arrived home, he was told that President Lincoln was waiting. But the general walked past the room where his guests waited, without saying anything, and went upstairs. A half hour later, Lincoln again told the porter he was waiting, but he was told the general had gone to sleep.

Hay was angry. He wrote in his diary, with considerable perception and foresight, probably just after getting back to the White House.

> I wish here to record what I consider a dreadful portent of evil to come. The President, Governor Seward and I went over to McClellan's house tonight. The Servant at the door said the General was at [a wedding] and would soon

return. We went in, and after we had waited about an hour McC. came in and without paying any particular attention to the porter who told him the President was waiting to see him, went upstairs, passing the door of the room where the President and Secretary of State were seated. They waited about half-an-hour, and sent once more a servant to tell the General they were there, and the answer came that the general had gone to bed.

I merely record this unparalleled insolence of epaulettes without comment. It is the first indication I have yet seen, of the threatened supremacy of the military authorities.

Coming home I spoke to the President about the matter but he seemed not to have noticed it specially, saying it was better at this time not to be making points of etiquette & personal dignity.[7]

Ulysses S. Grant, twenty years later, speculated that McClellan had a problem not from his age, but from not having had time to prepare for such an important and high-profile command. Grant said that McClellan had been given an almost impossible task. He thought McClellan might have done better had he worked his way up to prominence, as did Grant, William Sherman, George Thomas, and George Meade[8] (and, for that matter, Robert E. Lee and Thomas J. "Stonewall" Jackson).

McClellan's harshest critics accepted that he did an excellent job in organizing the Army of the Potomac. He also created a potentially effective overall strategy, based on Scott's groundwork—one properly calling for simultaneous advances of all Federal armies. The Confederates had the advantage of interior lines, enabling them to move troops to a threatened area as long as other areas remained quiet. If the Federals hit all fronts at once, Federal manpower advantage would come into play. The Confederates would not be able to reinforce endangered areas.

However, McClellan was far better at planning and organizing, and at declaring what he was going to do, than at actually doing. The modern phrase is that he talked the talk but could not walk the walk. McClellan was reluctant to even move his army, let alone use the army in combat. In March 1862, as a result, McClellan lost his job as general in chief. One can wonder, in the hindsight of 150 years, if Lincoln might have done better by taking advantage of McClellan's very real organizational and strategic skills, keeping him as general in chief but giving a more active general command of the Army of the Potomac.

McClellan, through arrogance, self-deception, lack of confidence, or any of the other reasons historians have suggested throughout the years since, failed to recognize and accept that political realities of the American Civil War required an appearance of action as well as action. McClellan provided neither, and resented Lincoln's suggestions, and orders, warning him and trying to get him to move.

McClellan operated in the military and political contexts of an entire war, not just of battles and their immediate campaigns. McClellan failed to realize that his actions, or lack of actions, annoying in themselves, were also being compared to the Federals in the West. In the West, the Federals enjoyed an almost unbroken string of success. A recent historian has summarized: "The military situation in the first half of 1862 followed a script decidedly favorable to the Union. Along the Mississippi River, United States forces made excellent progress toward the strategic goal, identified most famously by Winfield Scott in his so-called Anaconda Plan, of taking control of the great waterway and dividing the Confederacy into eastern and western parts."[9] Even the Battle of Shiloh, April 6 to 7, which for a day threatened to be a major Confederate victory, ended up a major Federal victory.

When this period ended, the only part of the Mississippi River—the main transportation artery of the area—the Confederates still controlled was the area between Baton Rouge and Vicksburg. But Federal control of the rest of the river effectively cut Confederate communications and supply over the Mississippi. Confederate policy, necessarily taking into account political as well as military realities, forced the Richmond government to try to defend all areas of the West. Even at the time some saw this as a mistake. The failure to muster all available troops to defend Middle Tennessee before the fall of Fort Henry and Fort Donelson in 1862, wrote Josiah Gorgas, Confederate ordnance chief, on June 12, 1862, "was the great mistake of the War."[10]

Little was different for the Confederates in Virginia. Joseph E. Johnston's ironically named Army of the Potomac withdrew south from the Manassas area on March 10, to near Fredericksburg, where the army would stay for about a month. That same day, receiving evidence that the Confederates were leaving, McClellan finally responded to a series of suggestions, and orders, from Lincoln and started his army toward Manassas.

When the Federals arrived at Manassas, they discovered that the Confederates had left behind much of their "artillery"—wooden "Quaker" guns, painted black in a successful effort to fool the Federal commanders about Confederate strength. A Pennsylvania soldier described finding these guns as "sickening" in that they had fooled the Northern commanders for months.[11] A civilian with the army wrote in his diary, "We have been humbugged by the rebels."[12] Bayard Taylor, reporting for the *New York Times*, wrote, "The fortifications are a complete humbug and McClellan has been completely fooled."[13]

Historian Stephen Sears writes that Allan Pinkerton, chief of army intelligence for McClellan, had reported the wooden guns six weeks before. Since McClellan had not planned to attack the Confederate emplacements around Manassas, wooden guns were as good as real guns.[14]

Later psychologists might have looked at the Union high command and commented, not for the last time, on people wanting to be fooled. McClellan was eight months into his tenure of always vastly overestimating the size of his opponent, as a reason, or an excuse, to spend more time preparing and less time acting. The element of sheer fear also cannot be discounted. Fear can paralyze as well as provoke action. "We become immobilized . . . many people become confused and unable to think clearly when they are scared."[15]

Lincoln held a cabinet meeting the next day, March 11. As one might expect, McClellan was the main topic of discussion. McClellan's arrogant inaction had managed to alienate most of his friends in the administration. The news from the other fronts, even from Hampton Roads, where the USS *Monitor* had managed to stalemate the CSS *Virginia*, was good, and stood in contrast to the sitzkreig—to use an anachronistic term—the sitting war on the Potomac. Lincoln was willing to overlook the Manassas embarrassment, realizing he had no alternative commander, but he concluded that McClellan could not function as Army of the Potomac commander and general in chief. McClellan was relieved of the latter assignment.

Lincoln asked William Dennison, former governor of Ohio and a friend of McClellan's from when McClellan commanded in Ohio, to break the news. McClellan was telegraphed to come back to Washington. McClellan first considered this some sort of plot by his enemies, and he refused to come to Washington. He read of his relief the next day in the newspapers, "proving," in McClellan's mind, his point. Dennison did get to McClellan's headquarters later and managed to convince the general that he still maintained Lincoln's confidence, and that Lincoln considered command of the primary army more important.

The nonmilitary context of this military campaign showed itself in the Washington legislative scene. The Republican Party made progress on its legislative agenda, possibly one of the most influential ever, in light of the 150 years since that time. The first seven months of 1862 saw the passage of the Homestead Act on May 20, distributing Federal lands in the West, what we now call the lower Midwest, to those willing to settle and work the land. Its influence would be felt after the Civil War. On July 2 and 3, Senator Justin Morrill's land grant college legislation, a transcontinental railroad bill, and an internal revenue bill were passed. The Republican vision of moving the United States toward the late nineteenth century as an industrial and agricultural giant, with, in a reversal of modern political party ideology, extensive Federal assistance and Federal taxes, driven by free labor, seemed to be on track.

Emancipation of black slaves was a major and divisive political issue in the North. Democrats, in general, loudly insisted they would risk lives and treasure to save the Union but not to free enslaved black people. The notion of striking at the South's social system by destroying slavery alienated Democrats, virtually all of whom would have seconded George B. McClellan's adamant opposition to adding freedom to the union as a Northern war aim.

In November 1861 McClellan wrote, "I am fighting to preserve the integrity of the Union & the power of the Govt—on no other issue. To gain that end we cannot afford to raise up the negro question—it must be incidental & subsidiary."[16] Democrats at the time failed to look at slavery as the foundation of the Southern economy and of the Southern ability to wage war. Economic warfare had not yet become a fully accepted method of waging war outside of the minds of the more radical Republican politicians and military leaders.

One expert on Democratic politics during the Civil War writes of the vigor with which the Democrats opposed many Republican policies, observing that the party "forcefully challenged the government's policies, particularly the administration's determination to use whatever means necessary to destroy the South and inflict blows against a social system in the name of winning the war."[17]

The Republican majority overcame Democratic opposition to preliminary civil rights legislation. In the immediate aftermath of McClellan's "Manassas campaign," on March 13, 1862, Congress passed legislation prohibiting the use of military power to return fugitive slaves to rebel owners. Southerners seemed to think that the North, in their view now a hostile foreign country with whom they were at war, should still help enforce Southern law. Republicans then found this argument as bizarre as it seems today, and passed the March 13 law to end the practice. The Republicans abolished slavery in the District of Columbia on April 16, and prohibited slavery in all Federal territories on June 19.

One Federal general, Benjamin Butler, came up with the interesting argument that freeing Southern slaves in occupied Southern territory was not jumping the gun on Federal policy. Rather, it was taking the Southerners at their word: that slaves were property, and was therefore seizing enemy property.

Black and white abolitionists, Radical Republicans, and some moderate Republicans supported more sweeping legislation. Abraham Lincoln, who wanted to control the issue himself, first began to consider calling for emancipation as a measure necessary to defeat the Confederacy.

McClellan's Richmond campaign served as a major wild card in this debate over emancipation. A Federal victory and the capture of Richmond, coming on the heels of so many Northern successes elsewhere, might convince white Southerners to abandon their cause. That in turn could end the war before the Federal government decided to insist on emancipation as a precondition to restoration of the Union. McClellan, not the most perceptive individual, actually seemed to appreciate this potential cause and effect. However, when the Peninsula campaign got underway, this would have unexpected results.

By March 13, 1862, McClellan had lost one of his two jobs, general in chief of the US Army, but remained in command of the Army of the Potomac. He finally seemed ready to move, though. McClellan had a plan to move his army down to the peninsula between the York and James Rivers, to Fort Monroe, and advance to take Richmond before the main Confederate army, now withdrawn to near Fredericksburg, could intercept him. McClellan's troops began to move south by ship on March 17, with the first men arriving a day or two later. The entire process would take three weeks, relatively quickly by the travel standards of the day.

On their arrival at Fort Monroe, McClellan's army would be roughly a seventy-five-mile march from Richmond, a little further from Richmond than Johnston's army at the time. Jefferson Davis's recently appointed military advisor, Robert E. Lee, effectively the equivalent of the modern chief of staff, did not know McClellan's overall plans. The early phases of the Federal movement to the peninsula might be a feint, to either distract attention from a direct attack on Johnston or to cause him to retreat southward, and clear the direct overland route for a Federal advance on Richmond. This initial Confederate confusion as to Federal intention served to counteract the defensive advantages they might get from the combination of the bad peninsula roads and poor Federal maps.

McClellan also preferred to wait for all his men to arrive at the Fort Monroe area, at the tip of a second, smaller peninsula shooting off from the first. Overcrowding alone, a major health hazard with the poor preventive health measures of the time, would have called for McClellan to advance as soon as a workable portion of his army had arrived. But this was not McClellan's way. McClellan himself arrived on April 3. On April 4, his army did begin to head north, until it came to Yorktown the next day, twenty miles north of Fort Monroe. Confederate entrenchments at Yorktown, partially based on British positions from the 1781 siege, stretched across the entire peninsula, itself only about ten miles wide.

McClellan, always likely to grossly overestimate the size of his opponents, outdid himself this time. McClellan had actually begun with a relatively accurate estimate of Confederate defenders at Yorktown, fifteen thousand, perhaps fifteen hundred above the actual total. But then a whole lot of things began to go wrong in McClellan's mind, and in reality. He began to use circular logic. As an experienced engineer officer, McClellan assumed that with a mere fifteen thousand men, the Confederates would not try to hold a defensive line. Since they were holding the line, therefore they had more than fifteen thousand men.

McClellan's natural tendency to inflate the odds against him was exacerbated by the Confederate commander. The Confederate commander on the scene did not just wait for McClellan's mind to do his work for him. McClellan was facing a Confederate commander very skilled at bluffing, a skill McClellan clearly lacked and could not appreciate. Major General John B. Magruder was known as "Prince" John Magruder for his flamboyant image. Magruder was also interested in the theater. He put on a good show here, added by intermittent clearings in the Confederate lines, visible from a distance from Federal lines. During the day, units would march through the clearings, visible to the Federals, return through the woods where they could not be seen, then march through the clearing again. Units could be counted several times. Troops would light extra campfires at night. Empty trains would arrive at night, to be greeted by cheering. Confederates in their trenches made it a point to shoot at, with rifles or cannon, any Federals who got close enough to take a careful look at their enemy's positions.

Allan Pinkerton, in charge of Federal intelligence efforts—and later the founder of the famous detective agency—consistently brought McClellan excessive estimates of enemy strength. Federal balloon observer Professor Thaddeus Lowe tried his best, but he was also fooled by Magruder. Lowe was not a trained soldier, and was not always able to correctly evaluate what he saw. But at Yorktown, he was not the only one with this problem. The net result was that not only did Magruder have substantially more than fifteen thousand men in McClellan's mind, but he also obviously was being reinforced by Johnston's main army. One can rarely come up with the correct answer by asking the wrong questions. McClellan was seeking ways to fight an enemy he saw with perhaps ten times its actual strength. Perversely, McClellan's caution sometimes makes sense, if he actually believed his inflated enemy strength estimates.

More factors came into play for McClellan. As a former army engineer, he was inclined toward a formal siege of Yorktown, whatever the enemy strength, and this took time. Siege artillery had to be brought to the scene, over what turned out to be very poor roads. A trench system had to be dug, moving closer and closer to the target. Things had to be done carefully. McClellan wrote to Flag Officer[18] Louis Goldsborough, "Our neighbors are in a very strong position. . . . I cannot turn Yorktown without a *battle* [italics in original], in which I must use heavy artillery & go through the preliminary operations of a siege."[19] Of course, formal siege operations were not designed for use where the enemy was only besieged on one side. One should also remember that, in a few weeks, McClellan would be facing, as his chief Confederate opponent, another former engineer officer.

A British observer had called McClellan's wide-ranging strategic sweep from Washington to Fort Monroe "the stride of a giant." He called the Yorktown siege, the second step in the campaign, "that of a dwarf."[20]

McClellan was also somewhat paranoid, though that particular term was not created until later. He thought the administration and the more radical abolitionist Republicans wanted him to fail. McClellan recognized that a capture of Richmond might end the Civil War right then and restore the Union the way it was—with no social changes, particularly with slavery intact. McClellan had made it clear that he was fighting only to preserve the Union.

On April 5, 1862, the day McClellan started his siege of Yorktown, he received a telegram from Washington. A large Federal corps at Fredericksburg, under Irwin McDowell, had been left to guard Washington and to watch Johnston's army. When Johnston's army headed south, McDowell's corps was supposed to do the same, hopefully to eventually hit the Confederate positions from the northeast, while McClellan came up from the southeast. But McDowell was now not going to join McClellan.

In McClellan's mind, this was proof that the Lincoln administration wanted him to fail and his army to lose. McClellan started complaining, to the White House and to his wife, about not being properly sustained. In one letter to his wife, a few days later, he wrote, "History will present a sad record of those traitors who are willing to sacrifice the country & its army for personal spite & personal aims. The people will soon understand the whole matter & then woe betide the guilty ones."[21] Historian Jeffry Wert puts it well in writing that "McClellan refused to see or admit his responsibility."[22]

In Lincoln's mind, withholding McDowell's corps was made necessary by McClellan's failure to carry out his orders to leave Washington sufficiently protected. Whether accidentally, by miscounting Federal troops in the area of D.C., or intentionally, McClellan did not leave what Lincoln considered sufficient manpower to prevent a Confederate thrust at the city. This is why Lincoln kept McDowell's thirty-eight thousand men where they were. Lincoln telegraphed McClellan on April 9:

MY DEAR SIR: Your dispatches complaining that you are not properly sustained, while they do not offend me, do pain me very much. Blenker's division was withdrawn from you before you left here, and you know the pressure under which I did it, and, as I thought, acquiesced in it—certainly not without reluctance.

After you left I ascertained that less than 20,000 unorganized men, without a single field battery, were all you designed to be left for the defense of Washington and Manassas Junction, and part of this even was to go to General Hooker's old position.

General Banks' corps, once designed for Manassas Junction, was diverted and tied up on the line of Winchester and Strasburg, and could not leave it without again exposing the Upper Potomac and the Baltimore and Ohio Railroad. This presented, or would present when McDowell and Sumner should be gone, a great temptation to the enemy to turn back from the Rappahannock and sack Washington. My explicit order that Washington should, by the judgment of all the commanders of army corps, be left entirely secure, had been neglected. It was precisely this that drove me to detain McDowell.

I do not forget that I was satisfied with your arrangement to leave Banks at Manassas Junction; but when that arrangement was broken up and nothing was substituted for it, of course I was constrained to substitute something for it myself. And allow me to ask, do you really think I should permit the line from Richmond via Manassas Junction to this city to be entirely open except what resistance could be presented by less than 20,000 unorganized troops? This is a question which the country will not allow me to evade.

There is a curious mystery about the number of troops now with you. When I telegraphed you on the 6th, saying you had over 100,000 with you, I had just obtained from the Secretary of War a statement, taken, as he said, from your own returns, making 108,000 then with you and *en route* to you. You now say you will have but 85,000 when all *en route* to you shall have reached you. How can the discrepancy of 23,000 be accounted for?

As to General Wool's command, I understand it is doing for you precisely what's [*sic*] like number of your own would have to do if that command was away. I suppose the whole force which has gone forward for you is with you by this time, and, if so, I think it is the precise time for you to strike a blow. By delay the enemy will relatively gain upon you—that is, he will gain faster by fortifications and re-enforcements than you can by re-enforcements alone. And once more let me tell you it is indispensable to you that you strike a blow. I am powerless to help this. You will do me the justice to remember I always insisted that going down the bay in search of a field, instead of fighting at or near Manassas, was only shifting and not surmounting a difficulty; that we would find the same enemy and the same or equal intrenchments at either place. The country will not fail to note, is now noting, that the present hesitation to move upon an intrenched enemy is but the story of Manassas repeated. I beg to assure you that I have never written you or spoken to you in greater kindness of feeling than now, nor with a fuller purpose to sustain you, so far as, in my most anxious judgment, I consistently can. But you must act.[23]

McClellan realized he had to keep going. By early May he finally had everything in place for his siege. On May 3, however, with McClellan's army in place between Yorktown and Richmond, Joseph Johnston ordered Yorktown evacuated. McClellan must have thought his cautious approach was working. The Federals did take the Yorktown lines. On May 5, a brief battle at Williamsburg held up the Federals long enough for Johnston to get his army back closer to Richmond.

McDowell's corps was now released from the Washington defenses and started south toward Richmond. Most, but not all, of the Confederate forces in Virginia were now defending Richmond. Johnston could not move to intercept McDowell without clearing the path for McClellan in so obvious a manner that even McClellan would move. If Johnston stayed where he was, McDowell would be able to capture Richmond.

Thomas J. "Stonewall" Jackson had a small force in the Shenandoah Valley, northwest of Richmond. He had already started military campaigns in the valley. Lee instructed him to increase his efforts, so he could act as a distraction for the Federals and a diversion of Federal troops from Richmond. Jackson had once complimented McClellan, telling a friend about McClellan that "if he can handle his troops in the field with the same ability with which he organizes them in camp, he will be simply invincible."[24]

Of course, Jackson was a totally different type of general than McClellan. In another discussion with the same friend, he said, "War means fighting. The business of a soldier is to fight. Armies are not called out to dig trenches . . . but to find the enemy, and strike him, to invade his country and do him all possible damage in the shortest possible time."[25] When the friend commented that this would be very destructive, Jackson responded, "Yes, while it lasted; but such a war would of necessity be of brief continuance, and so would be an economy of prosperity and life in the end."[26]

Jackson's campaign in the Valley would succeed in keeping reinforcements from McClellan, including McDowell's large force. Lincoln and Secretary of War Edwin Stanton may have overestimated the actual danger Jackson posed to Washington. Military decisions have never been, and likely never will be, totally reality based. However, it was a military decision taken in good faith that was the reason McClellan did not get the reinforcements he declared necessary for a successful campaign. But McClellan saw conspiracy when, at worst, he should have seen misjudgment. Dealing with reality, military and political, is the mark of a successful military commander.

By late May 1862, despite Confederate action, and despite "conspiracies" in Washington, McClellan and his army had almost reached the gates of Richmond. John Beauchamp Jones, a clerk in the War Department whose famous diary describes life in wartime Richmond, wrote about civilians impatient with a defensive strategy. He noted each of the milestones along the road that carried McClellan's army to Richmond without a major battle. On March 2, 1862, Jones had been impressed with Johnston's withdrawal from Manassas, writing that Johnston "certainly made a skillful retrograde movement in the face of the enemy at Manassas. He has been keeping McClellan and his 210,000 men at bay for a long time with about 40,000."[27]

By the eighth of May, Jones thought Johnston was overdoing the strategic withdrawal bit. That day he wrote, "Norfolk and Portsmouth are evacuated! Our Army falling back! The Merrimac is to be, or has been, blown up!"[28] Abraham Lincoln, down to visit McClellan at the start of the advance toward Richmond, had actually personally selected the site of a Federal landing near Norfolk.

Six days later Jones used fewer exclamation points in an equally dreary entry. "Our army has fallen back to within four miles of Richmond. Much anxiety is felt for the fate of the city. Is there no turning point in this long line of downward progress?"[29]

Joseph Johnston, commanding Confederate forces in Virginia, had withdrawn from Northern Virginia almost back to Richmond itself. Strategic retreat, a military if not a political option for the Confederates in the huge Western theater, was always difficult in the East. By late May, with the Federals six miles from Richmond, strategic withdrawal was no longer an option.

Johnston had to fight. Having discovered that McClellan's army was split by the Chickahominy River, Johnston attacked the smaller Federal force. The Battle of Seven Pines, or Fair Oaks, began. Under Johnston's very complicated plan, two-thirds of his army were supposed to attack Federal forces south of the river, the II and IV Corps. Four different Confederate columns were supposed to converge on Federal troops, using three different roads.

The battle plan, explained verbally to the subordinate Confederate commanders, fell apart almost immediately. James Longstreet's command took the wrong road, delaying the bulk of the Confederate attack.

The battle plan fell apart almost immediately. James Longstreet, instead of using the Nine Mile Road as ordered, moved down the Williamsburg Road, which had been assigned to D. H. Hill's and Benjamin Huger's troops, thus delaying the Confederate attack. Major General D. H. Hill started the fighting at 1:00 p.m. when his unsupported brigades struck Erasmus Keyes IV Corps positions at Seven Pines. The Federals were pushed back at this point. The Federals withdrew to a strong position when the fighting ended around 6:00 p.m.

The Confederate attack at the Fair Oaks sector began around 4:00 p.m. but failed to dent the Federal positions. Johnston, riding along his lines that evening, was seriously wounded. His senior subordinate, Major General G. W. Smith, took over.

Jefferson Davis and Robert E. Lee met with Smith the first night of the battle, to discuss Smith's plans for the next day. Confederate forces had made some progress in pushing back the Federals, despite trouble in coordinating their attacks, but the ultimate result of the battle remained undecided. Smith, however, did not seem to know how the battle had gone. He even asked Davis for information on what had happened. Smith himself later admitted that "Mr. Davis did not seem pleased with what I said."[30] Davis was more than displeased. He could not do so while the battle was on, but he had already decided to remove Smith from command of the army.

Smith continued the attack the next day, but he was driven back to the Confederate starting position. On the evening of June 1, at the end of the battle, Jefferson Davis rode out to visit Smith and the wounded Johnston. When Lee arrived at Smith's headquarters, a little after Davis, Smith had already been relieved of command. With no ceremony, Lee, like McClellan a former engineer officer, was offered and accepted command of the army. The next day, suffering from what today might be described as nervous exhaustion, or a nervous breakdown, and buckling under pressure of any command, Smith was relieved from active duty. His division was broken up, and Smith never held another field command.

Davis's choice of Lee was not totally popular. One writer, Richmond editor Edward A. Pollard, noted for lack of restraint in his writing, wrote about Lee's unsuccessful command in western Virginia and described him as "a general who had never fought a battle . . . and whose extreme tenderness of blood induced him to depend exclusively upon the resources of strategy, to essay the achievement of victories without the cost of life."[31]

Lee immediately renamed his army the Army of Northern Virginia, a way of symbolically showing where he wanted the army to operate—nearly one hundred miles to the north of where it was then entrenched. Lee then looked to grab the initiative. His enemies, and many of his fellow Confederates, would learn that seeking the initiative was perhaps the core element of Lee as a commander.

McClellan remained motionless but still virtually at the gates of Richmond. Lee pulled in as many men as he could, raising an army almost as large as McClellan's, the closest he would come in the war to matching his opponent's strength.

Earlier in the campaign, the frequently unperceptive McClellan told Lincoln that he had heard that Johnston was now under Lee's command—substantially true, since Lee, as military advisor to President Davis, could influence, if not directly command, Johnston's instructions. McClellan did not know that Lee was the one who had come up with the overall idea for Jackson's Shenandoah Valley campaign, though Jackson had brilliantly filled in the details. McClellan was encouraged when he thought Lee was in overall command. He told the president that "I prefer Lee to Johnston . . . [Lee] was too cautious & weak under grave responsibility . . . wanting in moral firmness when pressed by heavy responsibility & likely to be timed & irresolute in action." A few days later, McClellan added that "Lee will never venture upon a bold movement on a large scale."[32] Historian Stephen Sears points out that, fortunately for McClellan, these "interesting" observations were not made public while McClellan was still alive.[33] Sears, perhaps because McClellan made his observations early in the campaign, resists the temptation to comment that most of McClellan's statements, aside from the bold move to Fort Monroe, could apply to McClellan himself.

Lee lost or stalemated most of the series of battles that followed in the next week, collectively known as the "Seven Days Battles." Lee's plans were too complex, counting on intricate timing by separate commands. Lee was not communicating as well with his senior subordinates as he would later. Operations, coordinating separate and independent military units, were not as well developed an art then as later.

Stonewall Jackson was surprisingly slow, failing to keep to schedule during most of the battle. The only possible explanation was that days of little or no sleeping was catching up to this general normally known for speed. Jackson also had intricate knowledge of the geography and topography of the Shenandoah Valley, and had no such knowledge of the area near Richmond and the Peninsula.

McClellan never followed up his relative success. He preferred self-congratulations on how he was changing his base, from the York River to the James River, and not retreating, and how he was fighting off vastly superior enemy forces. At most, Lee had about 90 percent of McClellan's manpower. Lee, aided by McClellan's retreating after each battle, regardless of the results and the strength of the Federal position, forced McClellan back to the area of Fort Monroe, at the tip of the Virginia Peninsula. (The fact that the total effect of a campaign can be more important than individual battle results was a lesson not lost on Ulysses S. Grant.) Lee's context was to push the Federal army away from Richmond. Winning a battle is better than losing a battle, but as long as the Federals retreated Lee did not concern himself with the tactical results.

George McClellan was never one to accept responsibility, or even credit his enemies for doing their jobs, when there was someone to blame. Just about midnight on June 27, 1862, after a day's fighting at Mechanicsville, McClellan ended a telegram to Stanton with "If you save the Army now I tell you plainly that I owe no thanks to you or to any other persons in Washington—you have done your best to sacrifice this Army."[34] This telegram had an unusual effect. Rather than instantly costing McClellan his job, from McClellan's point of view nothing happened. McClellan took it as an example of the fact that though they would not support him as he felt he needed to be supported, the Lincoln administration would not dare to remove him from command. McClellan, however, had no way of knowing that the telegraph operator in Washington took it to his superior, who was horrified at the gross insubordination of the last lines. The last two sentences were removed before Stanton, and Lincoln, saw the message.

McClellan got back to safety at Harrison's Landing, and then Fort Monroe a few days later, to sit and sulk and to complain. Though McClellan remained popular with the bulk of his army, his reputation suffered among those officers and men in the army who believed he had retreated unnecessarily, giving up favorable ground after repelling Lee's attacks at Malvern Hill, the last major battle of the Seven Days, and badly botched a brilliant opportunity to capture the enemy's capital. No one expressed greater outrage at this result than Brigadier General Philip Kearny, the combative commander of the Third Division of Brigadier General Samuel P. Heintzelman's Third Corps. McClellan's cautious approach to warfare frustrated Kearny, who poured out his unhappiness in letters to his wife. Writing from Harrison's Landing on July 1, Kearny charged that "McClellan's treasons or mismanagement has thrown on us a great many partial Battles, of much severity, which he should have spared us. But all of which he invited by his bad arrangements."[35] Nine days later, Kearny claimed that "McClellan's want of Generalship, or treason, has gotten us into a place, where we are completely boxed up. . . . And out of which nothing short of most bold and dashing moves can extricate us to be of any service."[36]

Yet McClellan retained the confidence of most of his army. Many Federal soldiers believed their government had failed to provide the men and material necessary for victory. Frederick Law Olmsted, general director of the US Sanitary Commission (and the main designer of Central Park in New York City, Prospect Park in Brooklyn, and the landscaping of Capitol Hill in Washington, D.C.), spoke with officers and enlisted men at Harrison's Landing immediately after the Seven Days. Olmsted found that the army believed it had fought well against a superior foe and only needed reinforcements to go after the rebels again. Some in the army were "utterly despondent and fault-finding," but "there is less of this than ever before, and fewer stragglers and obvious cowards. . . . Of what we saw after Bull Run there is not the slightest symptom."[37] In a letter dated July 6, Olmsted urged Lincoln to send fifty thousand fresh men to the Army of the Potomac. "Without these," he observed pessimistically, "the best army the world ever saw must lie idle, and, in discouragement and dejection, be wasted by disease."[38]

The Richmond campaign exacerbated the distrust, never good to begin with, between conservative Democratic generals and Washington Republicans. McClellan gave Lincoln a letter when Lincoln visited him at Harrison's Landing, which called for the continuance of a restrained form of warfare against the Confederacy. Lincoln, however, was already beginning to think of the need for stronger measures—particularly emancipating Confederate slaves.

While McClellan sulked, Lee moved north, after a second Federal target.

3

McCLELLAN'S LAST STAND

Second Bull Run and Antietam

I shall not, however, soon forget the night; so dark, so obscure, so mysterious, so uncertain; with the occasional rapid volleys of pickets and outposts, the low, solemn sound of the command as troops came into position, and withal so sleepy that there was a half-dreamy sensation about it all; but with a certain impression that the morrow was to be great with the future fate of our country.

—General Alpheus Williams, September 1862[1]

Even before the end of the Seven Days Battles, the North put together a second main army in Virginia—the Army of Virginia—under Major General John Pope, to operate in Northern Virginia. With Stonewall Jackson having joined with Lee, Federal units from the Shenandoah Valley and McDowell's large corps were combined into this new army. John Pope, a general with some success under his belt, was brought in from the West to take command.

McClellan still claimed to be willing to go after Lee and Richmond. He asked for reinforcements, so that he would have a chance against the two hundred thousand Confederates he thought he was facing. Hearing this in person from McClellan, in a late July trip to the Peninsula, the new general in chief, Henry Halleck, concluded that "either no feasible reinforcement would give McClellan enough men to capture the Confederate capital, or that McClellan was so overawed by the enemy that there was no chance of his mustering the determination within himself to take it."[2] Twenty-twenty hindsight is not necessary to see that Halleck was right.

McClellan remained in command of the Army of the Potomac, when no alternative commander for the Army of the Potomac presented himself, but Lincoln, Stanton, and Halleck began, in August, to take some divisions from McClellan and send them to Pope.

Pope got off to a bad start on his arrival in Virginia. He issued the following proclamation to this new army.

HEADQUARTERS ARMY OF VIRGINIA,
Washington, D.C., July 14, 1862.
To the Officers and Soldiers of the Army of Virginia:

By special assignment of the President of the United States I have assumed the command of this army. I have spent two weeks in learning your whereabouts, your condition, and your wants, in preparing you for active operations, and in placing you in positions from which you can act promptly and to the purpose. These labors are nearly completed, and I am about to join you in the field.

Let us understand each other. I have come to you from the West, where we have always seen the backs of our enemies; from an army whose business it has been to seek the adversary and to beat him when he was found; whose policy has been attack and not defense. In but one instance has the enemy been able to place our Western armies in defensive attitude. I presume that I have been called here to pursue the same system and to lead you against the enemy. It is my purpose to do so, and that speedily. I am sure you long for an opportunity to win the distinction you are capable of achieving. That opportunity I shall endeavor to give you. Meantime I desire you to dismiss from your minds certain phrases, which I am sorry to find so much in vogue amongst you. I hear constantly of "taking strong positions and holding them," of "lines of retreat" and of "bases of supplies." Let us discard such ideas. The strongest position a soldier should desire to occupy is one from which he can most easily advance against the enemy. Let us study the probable lines of retreat of our opponents, and leave our own to take care of themselves. Let us look before us, and not behind. Success and glory are in the advance, disaster and shame lurk in the rear. Let us act on this understanding, and it is safe to predict that your banners shall be inscribed with many a glorious deed and that your names will be dear to your countrymen forever.

JNO. POPE[3]

After Pope finished insulting his own army, he got down to outraging local Confederate civilians. Pope added a new element to the Northern arsenal of weapons—direct efforts against the enemy population. There is no real evidence, though, of the Federal high command considering a deliberate policy of anything resembling twentieth-century-style total warfare. Pope's efforts were quite mild by the standards of modern warfare, and some even seem reasonable to current morality. However, they were a shock at the time, representing a significant "hardening" of the war. An effort against the base of support for the Confederate armies, Southern civilians, was now a weapon in the Northern arsenal. Strategically, this was not a bad idea. But Pope seemed to be making things hard for himself.

Three general orders, issued July 18, 1862, "set forth the methods by which [Pope] was determined to keep the citizens of occupied Virginia territory under strict control."[4] The Army of Virginia would "live off the land," to the extent possible, paying for requisitioned supplies with vouchers. As was made clear when the vouchers were issued, there was a major catch for any Southern sympathizer receiving a voucher. "Vouchers will be given to the owners, stating on their face that they will be payable at the conclusion of the war, upon sufficient testimony being furnished that such owners have been loyal citizens of the United States since the date of the vouchers."[5] The "rebels" who ignored Pope's opportunity to "repent" could say good-bye to their resources.

Southern citizens would be held responsible for damage to Federal railroad tracks, telegraph lines and roads, and for attacks on army supply wagon convoys and stragglers. Payment would consist of personally repairing the damage and paying, in money or property, the expenses of Federal troops enforcing these measures. Any person whose house was used to fire on Federal troops would have the house burned, and be arrested. Anyone caught firing on Federal troops would be shot.[6]

A few days later, General Order #11 called for all "disloyal male citizens" to be arrested and sent south, except for those willing to take a loyalty oath and furnish guarantees of good behavior. "If any person, having taken the oath of allegiance as above specified, be found to have violated it, he shall be shot, and his property seized and applied to the public use."[7]

Forty years ago, a historian summarized Pope's reasoning and the practical effort of his measures, by writing:

> There was no doubt that Pope believed strongly in the strictest kind of martial law in occupied territory. Doubtless his intent was to intimidate the Southerners as a preventive measure to effect economy in his own operations, on the premise that his troops would thus be more secure and would not be diverted from essential military operations by excessive police duties. While his purpose may have been militarily justified, the psychology was defective, for his

harsh measures only served to harden the resistance and strengthen the will of Confederate citizens to outsmart the invaders at every opportunity.[8]

Pope himself had to issue General Orders Number 19, toning down the enforcement of his General Orders No 5. "It is to be distinctly understood that neither officer nor soldier has any right whatever, under the provisions of that order, to enter the house, molest the persons, or disturb the property of any citizen whatsoever."[9] Some of Pope's men seemed to be overdoing their commander's intent.

Force must have focus and control, and even Pope thought his measures might be getting out of hand. More importantly, Pope failed to carry out the key element in suppressing civilian resistance to an invading army—defeating the defending army. Lee's most able subordinate, Stonewall Jackson, carried out Lee's intention that "I want Pope to be suppressed."[10] In a movement of the type for which his campaign in the Shenandoah Valley, a few months before, had made him famous, and most unlike his lethargic performance in the Seven Days Battles a few weeks before, Jackson swung around the flank of Pope's army. Jackson defeated part of Pope's army at the Battle of Cedar Mountain. Pope's entire army, augmented by units of the Army of the Potomac (with McClellan's allegedly limited cooperation), after another Jackson wide flank movement, was beaten at the Second Battle of Bull Run.

The initiative in the East had fully shifted to Lee. In the pattern for which he was already becoming famous, Lee looked for a way to act on this opportunity. A few days after the Battle of Second Manassas (to give the Southern victory its Southern name), Lee wrote President Davis suggesting his army cross the Potomac into Union territory.

> The present seems to be the most propitious time since the commencement of the war for the Confederate Army to enter Maryland. The two grand armies of the United States that have been operating in Virginia, though now united, are much weakened and demoralized. Their new levies, of which I understand 60,000 men have already been posted in Washington, are not yet organized, and will take some time to prepare for the field. If it is ever desired to give material aid to Maryland and afford her an opportunity of throwing off the oppression to which she is now subject, this would seem the most favorable.[11]

Lee conceded the many logistical and supply problems, and a particularly severe manpower shortage, he would face in the incursion, but he argued against a static defense. Lee considered the risks of the campaign to be worth taking. The proposed campaign would defend Richmond by drawing the main Federal army far away from Richmond. Northern Virginia would also get a rest from the armies, and the Southern army could collect supplies from Northern territory untouched by war. Lee thought his offensive might fuel pro-Confederate sentiment in Maryland—though western Maryland was pro-Union, unlike the eastern part of the state. Finally, a successful Confederate offensive in the East, particularly if it included victory in a major battle, coupled with plans for a near-simultaneous advance by Southern armies in the West into Kentucky and Ohio, might convince European leaders, especially Britain, to recognize the Confederacy.

One result of the Seven Days Campaign, and McClellan's being turned away from Richmond, had been to call foreign attention to the war and the possibility of a Confederate victory. At the very least, a successful invasion of Northern soil would hurt the Republicans in the fall elections. Lee thought that Confederate success north of the Potomac River, particularly if he was still securely there when fall elections began in October, "would enable the people of the United States to determine at their coming elections whether they will support those who favor a prolongation of the war, or those who wish to bring it to a termination."[12]

Lee could not know another reason favoring invasion of the North at that time. Abraham Lincoln's issuance of the Emancipation Proclamation was on hold, at the suggestion of his cabinet, until the Federals could win a victory. A major Federal defeat, on Federal territory, at the very least would have postponed the Proclamation's issuance.

Lee wrote Davis that a major mitigation of the invasion's risk would be the demoralized state of the two Federal armies he had recently defeated. What is interesting and significant about Lee's arguments is that he considered the state of the enemy armies to be the primary factor justifying the campaign. "It is revealing that Lee's first consideration should be the condition of his opponents, and even more revealing that he was willing to act upon his perception of their weakness,"[13] to quote a 1999 study of the campaign. Most of Lee's early Federal opponents would never have thought about Confederate weaknesses, only their own. Lee himself was always a "force multiplier" for the Confederates, in the constant Federal tendency to overestimate his army's strength and in the Federal tendency to believe Lee (and Jackson) capable of military feats even greater than their actual considerable ability.

Lee's innate preference for the offensive may have been the final and deciding element in his decision to head north. He chose to go with the major benefits that could accrue from moving into Maryland and to put aside, as much as possible, the considerable risks. Incursion into the North was risky.

A Confederate victory in Maryland could go a long way toward convincing the Northern public that the war could not be won, at least not at an acceptable cost. A Confederate defeat, however, was possible and could be a major disaster away from home, with the Potomac River between Lee and his army and the relative safety of Virginia.

Lee knew the dangers at the time. After the war, a former Confederate staff officer reported Lee as saying, referring to criticisms about the great risk he had taken, "that such criticisms were obvious, but that the disparity of forces between the contending armies rendered the risks unavoidable."[14]

Confederate movement into Maryland was primarily aimed at forcing a battle with the Federal army, at a time and a place of Lee's choosing. Had the Federals chosen to carefully examine Lee's style as a general, they might have detected, even then, a major flaw amid the technical excellence—Lee likely attacked too often. Initiative does not necessarily mean taking the tactical offensive. Shaping a battle does not always mean firing the first shot. Rather, shaping a battle is better defined as fighting the battle on the commander's terms, not on those of his enemy. Second Bull Run is about Lee's only such battle, where he forced the Army of the Potomac to attack him at a place of his choosing rather than settling on a place he thought he could defend. Lee held his enemy in place by the initial phase of the fighting until he brought up James Longstreet's corps to deliver the blow that won the battle.

Lee's army began crossing into Maryland at White's Ford, on September 4, 1862, taking three days to get his army across. Lee rode in an ambulance, having injured both of his hands the last day of August. He could not mount his horse. Lee crossed the Potomac with roughly fifty-five thousand men, but these numbers quickly began to decline as men began to desert. Many thought they had signed up only to defend Virginia, and thus did not have to take part in the invasion of another state.

Stonewall Jackson had also been slightly injured at the start of the campaign, and he did not ride a horse into Maryland. Jackson was back on his horse by the time his corps reached Frederick, Maryland, the site of the "famous" Barbara Frietchie incident, where an old woman supposedly confronted Jackson, on his horse, and his men over her refusal to lower the American flag, which did not take place. This story began to circulate early in the campaign, however. Even before the Battle of Antietam, a Federal general looked into the incident, to discover it was not true, but he did persuade Frietchie to sell him another flag she had in her house.[15] Jackson's aide, Henry Kyd Douglas, later wrote that though there was a very old lady named Barbara Frietchie in Frederick, age ninety-nine, "She never saw Stonewall Jackson and he never saw her. I was with him every minute while he was in town, and nothing like the patriotic incident so graphically described by Mr. Whittier in his poem every occurred."[16] In fact, Douglas continued, Frietchie was a Confederate sympathizer. However, aided by John Greenleaf Whittier's talent, an early example of the power of media, the story of the brave old woman confronting the fierce general has gone down in history.

George McClellan had not actually been relieved of command of the Army of the Potomac after the Peninsula Campaign ended. However, most of his troops had either been shipped to John Pope's army or were on their way when Second Bull Run occurred. On September 2, 1862, however, that army was abolished and the troops reincorporated into the Army of the Potomac. Pope was sent to the Department of the Northwest to fight Indians. McClellan was put in charge of the Washington, D.C. defenses and all the troops available for the defense of Washington.

The question of field command remained unsettled. On September 3, Lincoln drafted an order, to be signed by Secretary of War Edwin Stanton, for General in Chief Henry Halleck to prepare a force for active operations. The implication was that Lincoln wanted Halleck to command the army himself. Halleck, however, a good general if properly directed but not likely to show much initiative, did not take the hint. A meeting on the morning of September 5 apparently confirmed McClellan as field commander, though how remains unclear. Possibly he was just reaffirmed as commander of the Army of the Potomac, which certainly allowed him to campaign with the army.

By late on Friday, September 5, McClellan began moving his troops northwest into Maryland in pursuit of Lee. On September 9, 1862, gambling on McClellan's lack of aggressiveness, Lee split his army. Jackson took roughly half the army to attempt to capture Harpers Ferry and the 12,500-man Federal garrison. Lee wrote out Special Order No. 191, detailing the positions and movements of all elements of the Army of Northern Virginia. Movements began on September 10. Unfortunately for the Confederates, someone lost a copy of the order. On September 13, Union soldiers found a copy of the order in an abandoned Confederate camp, wrapped around three cigars.

The Federal soldiers first noticed the cigars, but then noticed the wrapper. They took it to their company commander, who quickly sent the document up the chain of command. Their division adjutant general recognized the handwriting in the document as belonging to Lee's adjutant general, Robert H. Chilton, a comrade from the prewar army. He went to the acting commander of the XII Corp, who sent the documents on to McClellan. McClellan took one look at the document, and exclaimed, "Now I know what to do."[17]

There is no evidence that McClellan believed the orders to be a plant.[18] This may be too modern a thought, though at least as far back as George Washington American commanders recognized the advantage of giving false information to an enemy.[19] McClellan began to move quickly, for him, "though certainly more slowly than Lee would have moved in similar circumstances."[20] McClellan still thought he was facing an enemy army far larger than his own. As Bruce Catton put it, in McClellan's mind "the Federal army was outnumbered; the offensive thrust which he must presently make, to drive the invader back below the Potomac, was an enormously risky venture."[21]

McClellan defeated part of Lee's army on September 14 in the Battle of South Mountain, pushing them westward out of several passes. The next morning, on hearing that Harpers Ferry was to be surrendered, Lee ordered his army to concentrate near Sharpsburg, Maryland, just north of the Potomac, about fifteen miles west of Harpers Ferry.

Lee's men began to arrive at Sharpsburg on September 15, though it would be another day before the bulk of the army arrived. The first Federal divisions arrived the same evening, going into position across Antietam Creek from Lee. Estimates are that by the morning of September 16 Lee had fifteen thousand men immediately with him, confronting sixty thousand men immediately available to McClellan.

McClellan, in keeping with his nature, took things slowly and carefully, spending the day studying Confederate positions and waiting for more of his men to arrive. An officer from Maine wrote the next day that about 1 p.m., he heard cheers from the Federal ranks as McClellan rode past the troops. He continued to say that the cheering that greeted McClellan "was one continual roar. Satisfaction and confidence seemed stamped upon his continence."[22] A more cynical veteran commented, "No fight to-day; Little Mac has gone to the front. Look out for a fight when he goes to the rear."[23] Even at the heights of his popularity, there were those in the army who, if they did not dislike McClellan, recognized his faults. One can argue that the front line was not the place for the commander of a Civil War army; that presuming he can get sufficient information from the front he should be in the rear managing the battle. But a general should never have the reputation of one who avoids being where the action is. McClellan had started to develop that reputation.

Lee's position was defensible, but he had few men to hold the position and no place to retreat in case of defeat. Lee put on a bold front, bluffing McClellan into delaying the attack on September 15 and September 16. Jackson arrived on the 16th, with most of his men, but still giving Lee at most thirty-five thousand men to fight off eighty-five thousand Federals in the immediate vicinity—McClellan also had been reinforced.

McClellan thought the low hills making up the foundation of the Confederate position were too strong to attack directly. The plan McClellan communicated to several of his generals was to attack on both the Confederate left and right while feinting in the center. The attack in the center could become a full-fledged assault if the opportunity presented itself, if Lee weakened that area to defend his flanks.

However, the Federal commanders quickly grew confused. Ambrose Burnside, commanding on the Federal left, apparently did not understand that McClellan wanted simultaneous attacks on both flanks. After an inconclusive discussion with McClellan the afternoon of the 16th, Burnside apparently thought all McClellan wanted the next day was a diversion. McClellan's report, written about a month after the battle, is itself a little confusing in describing his plans:

> The design was to make the main attack upon the enemy's left—at least to create a diversion in favor of the main attack, with the hope of something more by assailing the enemy's right—and, as soon as one or both of the flank movements were fully successful, to attack their center with any reserve I might then have on hand.[24]

McClellan had the manpower to stage a coordinated attack and quickly finish off Lee's army. He had a plan that, had he ensured it was carried out as intended, might have worked, and might have won the North an overwhelming victory and finished the war right there. However, McClellan allowed his subordinates to attack one sector at a time, totally failing to achieve tactical coordination of efforts.

That night, as a modern historian puts it, "For the first time in McClellan's career, the Army of the Potomac prepared to launch a major [tactical] offensive against the Army of Northern Virginia."[25] The men knew a major battle was impending, and it should be assumed that few got much sleep that night. General Alpheus Williams, a division commander from the XII Corps, wrote his daughters a few days later, "I shall not, however, soon forget the night; so dark, so obscure, so mysterious, so uncertain; with the occasional rapid volleys of pickets and outposts, the low, solemn sound of the command as troops came into position, and withal so sleepy that there was a half-dreamy sensation about it all; but with a certain impression that the morrow was to be great with the future fate of our country."[26]

The bloodiest single day in American history, September 17, 1862, resulted in more than twice the dead of September 11, 2001[27] (though all the casualties at Antietam had known they were in harm's way). The fighting began about 6 a.m. with a Federal advance against the Confederate left. Joseph Hooker's I Corps, having crossed the Antietam the evening before, struck south against Stonewall Jackson's men on the Confederate left wing.

Hooker's lead units fought in an area known ever since as "The Cornfield." The high corn would have blocked soldiers' vision of their enemy but provided absolutely no protection from enemy fire. The Texas Brigade, part of a two-brigade division under John Bell Hood, had been relieved from the front line the evening of the 16th and were given permission to go to the rear for food. The only condition was that Hood had to specifically promise Stonewall Jackson that if the men were needed to come to the relief of the units relieving them, they would come immediately. Hood's men were needed.

After several hours of fierce back-and-forth fighting, the Federal attacks against the Confederate left ended with an uncoordinated attack by the II Corps. William French's division, II Corps, was misdirected when ordered to assist John Sedgwick's division in the attack on the left and ended up striking the Confederate center and shifting the focus of action. Lafayette McLaws's Confederate division was able to hit Sedgwick's flank, blunting the attack and causing heavy Federal casualties. Confederate troops had been drawn from their center and right. The failure of Sedgwick's attack, though, made success on the Federal right unlikely.

The story was different in the center. Federal efforts against the Confederate center began almost by accident, with French's attack. Federal attacks, particularly at a sunken road that later became known as Bloody Lane, were stopped almost at the point of success.

Photos of Bloody Lane, taken a few days later by Alexander Gardner, show a depression in the ground, if not literally covered with bodies, obviously showing the signs of heavy combat.[28] A Northern newspaper correspondent, visiting Bloody Lane the day after the battle, noted that Confederate bodies in the lane "were lying in rows like the ties of a railroad, in heaps, like cord-wood mingled with the splintered and shattered fence rails. Words are inadequate to portray the scene."[29]

There are some unusual ground features at Bloody Lane. Attacking Federal soldiers would have come over a hill, right into the face of the Confederate lines, perhaps seventy-five yards away. Here, the Federals suffered heavy casualties. The Confederate lines seemed to be holding at this point, but they were also taking heavy casualties. And part of the sunken road was less deep than elsewhere. A small knoll also overlooked this section. The knoll was high enough to enable forces holding it to shoot downward into the lane. Two Federal regiments, the 61st and 64th New York, both commanded that day by Colonel Francis Barlow, took the knoll. They were close to the enemy, shooting downward, and into the Confederate flank. Brigadier General Robert Rodes ordered one of his regiments to bend around to meet the Federal threat.

The regiment's commander got the message wrong, and pulled his men out of the line and headed to the rear. By the time Rodes could stop the withdrawal, it was too late. The other Confederates in the road had no choice but to retreat. The Federals soon took control of the sunken road.

However, a Confederate counterattack, and the death of the Federal division commander on the scene, Major General Israel Richardson, caused a loss of Federal momentum. McClellan, not in touch with his battle lines, failed to recognize and to exploit his success. Union troops in the center were ordered to hold their position, not to advance. Lee could repair the break in his lines.

McClellan's third effort was directed against Lee's right. McClellan was later criticized for his failure to consider a coordinated effort against all sectors of Lee's army, enabling Lee to expertly move troops to where they were needed. However, McClellan had ordered an attack on the Confederate right simultaneously with that on the left. He had planned, though he did not ensure, tactical coordination. (His job was to ensure coordination.) Major General Ambrose Burnside, planning only for a diversion, had neglected to fully reconnoiter the ground over which his men would have to attack. Additionally, a confusing command system had Burnside functioning as commander of this wing of the Federal army, with Jacob Cox commanding the IX Corps, the only troops in Burnside's wing.

Burnside and Cox had learned of a ford downstream from the main bridge in the area. Isaac Rodman's division was trying to find the ford while other Federal troops were trying to storm the bridge and taking heavy casualties. A small Confederate brigade, under Robert Toombs, held high ground with a clear line of fire to the bridge. Burnside gave evidence of his inflexibility as a commander by ordering the attacks to continue at the bridge, even when he saw nothing was being accomplished. The main IX Corps attack, once the Federals had managed to cross Antietam Creek, did not start until 3 p.m. The rest of the field was quiet by this time.

The Federal attack initially went well, though, pushing the Confederates right back through the streets of Sharpsburg. About 4:30 p.m., however, this changed when A. P. Hill's Confederate division arrived, after a seventeen-mile march from Harpers Ferry, where it had been paroling twelve thousand captured Federal troops—only at Bataan, in 1942, did a larger American force surrender. Hill's men slammed into Burnside's left flank, stopping its progress and forcing Federal troops back nearly to what soon would become known as Burnside Bridge. McClellan then seemed to fold his cards.

Hill's attack on Burnside's IX Corps disrupted Burnside's momentum, but it only hit the left of Burnside's corps. The right of the corps might have been able to hold in place, keeping Hill from pushing them back any further, and been used as the foundation for Federal reinforcements and another Federal thrust. Burnside did need some help to hold, and McClellan could see this from his headquarters on a hill behind Federal lines, even before Burnside's messenger arrived.

McClellan seems to have considered sending reinforcements. George A. Smalley, a reporter for the newspaper the *New York Tribune*, had stationed himself at McClellan's headquarters. In his article two days later, Smalley wrote about McClellan, "He sees clearly enough that Burnside is pressed—needs no messenger to tell him that. His face grows darker with anxious thought."[30] Smalley then saw McClellan look at the V Corps, held in reserve near headquarters. McClellan then looked at V Corps Commander Fitz John Porter, a friend of his. "But Porter slowly shakes his head, and one may believe the same thought is passing through the minds of both generals. They are the only reserves of the army; they cannot be spared.'"[31]

Smalley was with the two generals as they rode toward the left flank, and ran into Burnside's courier. The courier reported that Burnside needed more men and artillery immediately; otherwise he could not hold half an hour. After a moment's thought, McClellan replied, "Tell General Burnside this is the battle of the war. He must hold his ground till dark at any cost. I will send him Miller's battery. I can do no more. I have no infantry." Then, as the courier rode away, McClellan added, "Tell him if he cannot hold his ground, then the bridge, to the last man!—always the bridge! If the bridge is lost, all is lost!'"[32]

Burnside could hold ground just in front of the bridge. Hill's attack had blunted Burnside's, and caused several times as many casualties as it suffered. But Hill's force was too damaged to push any further.

No further Federal attacks followed, though at least twenty thousand Federal troops sat idle near the battlefield. (The next day McClellan received thirteen thousand reinforcements.)

Confederate General James Longstreet later wrote, "We were so badly crushed at the close of the day that ten thousand fresh troops could have come in and taken Lee's army and everything in it."[33]

Not under McClellan, however. The man always operated under the principle that Lee outnumbered him—even at Antietam, when Lee had an army less than half McClellan's size.

The Battle of Antietam, the bloodiest day in American history—roughly twenty-three thousand casualties on both sides—was over. The armies glowered at each other the next day, including the thirty thousand or more fresh Federal troops. McClellan never considered an attack that day, September 18, 1862, and allowed Lee to slip back over the Potomac.

Reaction to McClellan's failure to renew the offensive was mixed. Antietam was a unique experience for the Army of the Potomac. It was the largest and bloodiest battle so far fought in the East. The only comparable Western battle was Shiloh. Antietam was also the first battle in which the Army of the Potomac remained in place after the fighting ended. After their other battles, the army had either retreated or, occasionally, advanced. Here, for the first time, they could see, and hear, the horrible results of a battle. One junior officer wrote about the unpleasant uniqueness of the experience. "All hands agree that before they had never seen such a fearful battle."[34] A soldier from Connecticut later wrote of the night of September 17, 1862, "Of all gloomy nights, this was the saddest we ever experienced."[35]

Initially, in the immediate aftermath of the battle, the men tended to support McClellan's decision not to renew the attack. Alexander Webb, who eventually became a general, wrote, "Now that it is all over you will hear that we ought to have advanced the next day. Well I say that myself but no one thought so at the time. . . . I know of no advocates for a continuance of the battle on the 18th."[36] General George Meade wrote his wife that "our army was a good deal broken and demoralized—so much so that it was deemed hazardous to risk an offensive movement"[37] without reinforcements (which actually had arrived). The Federals, including their commander, could easily see the damage they had suffered. That the Confederates had suffered as much, or more, considering the much smaller size of their army, was hard to conceive with the Federal mindset of that period of the war.

A young officer, in a diary published much later, was harsher than Meade. The officer wrote, "Lee's army ought not to have gotten away so easily, but should have been pushed to the wall, and fought without mercy every day. From experience, however, we know that General McClellan is not equal to great occasions, and there it is useless to expect brilliant results while he is in command."[38]

What was interesting in the criticism of the actions of the army, and its failing to finish Lee off, is that though most commentators questioned the slow pursuit, they seemed not to blame the problems on McClellan, the army's commander. Fault tended to be placed on subordinate commanders, interfering politicians, and the press. The army, however, was willing to fight if the fighting did some good.

Two significant results followed from the Battle of Antietam. On November 7, 1862, Lincoln had finally had enough of McClellan. A final provocation may have been a telegram that McClellan sent to Lincoln in late October 1862 complaining about tired horses. Lincoln immediately wired back, "I have just read your dispatch about sore-tongued and fatigued horses. Will you pardon me for asking what the horses of your army have done since the battle of Antietam that fatigues anything?"[39]

The day after the November 1862 elections, having failed Lincoln's test to move to intercept Lee, McClellan was removed from command. He was sent home to New Jersey to await orders that never came. Ambrose Burnside, "painfully conscious that he was not qualified to command the army,"[40] was put in command. A few days later, Burnside told General in Chief Halleck, "I am not fit for [the command]. There are many more men in the army better fitted than I am; but, if you and the President insist, I will take it and do the best I can."[41]

The news was generally not taken well in the Army of the Potomac, where McClellan was popular, but there was no real effort to resist the orders. As to the new commander, the good news, in the old saying, was that Burnside was an appealingly modest commander in an era of prima donnas. The bad news was that he was correct in that he was not qualified to command an army.

The far more important result of the Battle of Antietam took place on September 22, 1862. This result makes the tactically stalemated battle one of the most decisive battles in history. Lincoln issued the preliminary Emancipation Proclamation. As of January 1, 1863, all slaves in areas still in rebellion would be free. Few slaves were freed—this would come later. However, the Proclamation put the North firmly on the side of freedom and against slavery. Compromise at home became impossible, and the war would be fought to the end. Blacks would become available as potential Federal soldiers, and 180,000 would eventually fight for the North. European, primarily British, recognition of the Confederacy or intervention to settle the war, would become far more difficult. This, however, initially was not for the commonly accepted reason.

Emancipation was seen by the British government as likely to lead to a bloody slave rebellion. Their government moved closer to intervention, for a time. Then, British Secretary of State for War George Cornwall Lewis, in a November 1862 memo to the Cabinet, pointed out the serious risks in intervention. Lewis pointed out that Britain was in a position analogous to France in 1778, when French recognition of the United States led to a major war with Britain.

British intervention might sustain the South, but holding Canada, particularly in winter when supply and reinforcement from Britain would be extremely difficult, against a large and vengeful American army would be uncertain. Lewis also wondered how wooden British and French warships would fare against Federal ironclads. Lewis raised the issue of the depth of feeling on both sides of the war, particularly after the Emancipation Proclamation ensured the war would be a total war, doubting any compromise was possible. The British government decided it was not prepared to risk a major war with the United States on behalf of a slave republic.

The best chance the Confederates had for outside aid was gone. Their only hope for winning the war lay in their own efforts to prevent the Union from meeting its conditions for victory. Lee's army became seen as the primary means of fending off Federal efforts. One dispatch, filed in late September, from a Confederate correspondent declared, "The army in Virginia stands guard this day, as it will stand guard this winter, over every hearthstone throughout the South. The ragged sentinel who may pace his weary rounds this winter on the bleak spurs of the Blue Ridge, or along the frozen valleys of the Shenandoah and Rappahannock, will also be your sentinel, my friend, at home."[42]

A modern historian explains the meaning of Lee's army to the South, and the implied reason the Eastern theater was now, most assuredly, the primary theater of war:

> In the space of less than three months, the Confederate people had come to expect good news from the Army of Northern Virginia, investing ever more emotional capital in its leaders and soldiers. That investment led to a belief in popular victory that would be as important as any other factor in lengthening the life of the Confederacy.[43]

4

CHANGING COMMANDERS, TWICE

I do not think it possible that such a change could have taken place for the better as has been effected in the short space of two months.

—Edmund English, Sergeant,
2nd New Jersey Volunteer Infantry, 1863[1]

The Democrats gained heavily in the fall 1862 elections, but not as much as Lincoln had feared. By November, elections were over, and any political reasons to keep George McClellan (a Democrat) in command of the Army of the Potomac were gone. McClellan was relieved of command and sent home to New Jersey to await orders. These orders never came. McClellan's replacement in command was Ambrose Burnside. Burnside had been offered the command before and turned it down. He had said he was not qualified to command an army.

Ambrose Burnside is known to those with an interest in the American Civil War and in military history. His name is known to the public for another reason, though they may not realize it. Though only thirty-eight when he took over command of the Army of the Potomac, Burnside was mostly bald. However, he had an awesome set of whiskers, stretching thickly to the base of his clean-shaven chin and then connecting to a thick mustache. They became known as burnsides, which evolved into the more logical-sounding sideburns.

Historians have a problem evaluating Burnside's promotion considering the results of his service as commander of the Army of the Potomac. Burnside had not done well at Antietam. He was slow to put his men in motion, despite McClellan's desire for a coordinated attack. He then insisted on stubbornly trying to get his men across what has become known as Burnside Bridge, rather than use an attack on the bridge as a diversion while his men looked for, and eventually found, a ford further down Antietam Creek. Burnside should have looked for the ford the day before. Later, even when A. P. Hill's men hit, and crumpled, Burnside's left flank, at least half of his attacking column was still in good shape and might have continued to attack or hold their gains, so, particularly if he had been reinforced, Burnside might have been able to renew his attack.

However, at least some of Burnside's problems could also be blamed on McClellan's failure to prod him and then back him up. Burnside had done well in his earlier independent command in North Carolina.

Burnside's appointment was political, though not in the usual sense. Burnside did not play politics. Lincoln had lost patience with McClellan and wanted to find as opposite a commanding general as possible. He thought he had such a man in Burnside.

At least one historian has pointed out how many observers seemed to remember being unhappy with Burnside's appointment, but that much of this was in retrospect.[2] "Despite the distorted recollections of some participants and the occasionally bizarre interpretations of subsequent students, Burnside's ascension to command did not cast an immediate pall over the entire army. "'We are well pleased with Burnside,' said a captain in the 'Iron Brigade' a fortnight after the change of command."[3]

Whatever doubts would soon emerge about Burnside's abilities as a commander, he was a popular figure. After graduating West Point in 1847, Burnside was sent to Mexico. On the way, he gambled away his passage money on a steamboat and had to borrow to finish the trip. "Later, in Mexico City, he played cards so enthusiastically and unskillfully that his pay was in hock for six months in advance, and he would have had to resign in disgrace if a senior officer had not loaned him enough to pay up."[4]

Burnside invented a breech-loading rifle in 1852, and he resigned from the army to try to market the gun. He went broke when a War Department contract fell through at the last moment. George McClellan, who had resigned from the army to become vice president of the Illinois Central Railroad, bailed out Burnside by giving him a job with the railroad's land office. (Interestingly, Abraham Lincoln did some legal work for the same railroad.)

There is a trap in writing history based on small signs of character, particularly since their meaning, if any, can only become clear in retrospect. However, McClellan had already shown how little one could accomplish, whatever one's skills, with lack of enthusiasm and confidence. It remained to be seen what Burnside could accomplish. Could his enthusiasm correct any failing in basic military skill?

Burnside got off to a good start. He seemed to come up with some good strategic ideas. Burnside outflanked Lee by moving the Army of the Potomac, still near Antietam, to just across the Rappahannock River from Fredericksburg. If Burnside could cross the river, his army would be between Lee and Richmond, with a clear shot at the Confederate capital. This was a plan with good potential, from a general usually not associated with good plans. Then things began to go wrong.

The first elements of the Army of the Potomac arrived across from Fredericksburg on November 17, 1862, with the bulk of the army arriving days later. Unfortunately, the Rappahannock is not fordable at that point under the best of circumstances. Heavy rains were making the river even harder to cross. The pontoons, to be used to bridge the river, did not arrive until November 24. General in Chief Henry Halleck had not told his chief engineer—though one supposes the engineer should have guessed—how urgent the matter was. The engineers struggling to get the pontoons down to Fredericksburg had no idea they should be in a hurry. Neither Halleck nor Burnside pushed sufficiently to get the pontoons to Fredericksburg on time.

Soon after taking command, Burnside divided the army corps into three "grand divisions." What was called the Right Grand Division was placed under the command of Edwin V. Sumner, a veteran of about forty years' service in the army. The Center Grand Division went to Joseph Hooker. The Left Grand Division went to William Franklin. A fourth reserve, Grand Division, was formed from the XI and XII Corps and given to Franz Sigel. This grand division covered Washington, D.C., and Harpers Ferry.

The military term *operations* can loosely be defined as coordinating different and independent elements. Operations can be called the first active step in carrying out strategic plans. Operations were not turning out to be one of Burnside's strengths. Neither was improvising, quickly coming up with Plan B when Plan A is no longer feasible.

John Edmond Gough, a British brigadier general killed in action in World War I, wrote about Burnside and his plan in 1913.

Apart from the fact that a commander worth of his sale does not allow his plans to be frustrated by matters of this sort, there is a lesson to be learnt which should be carefully noted by all officers. Avoid planning which depends upon *everything* panning out *exactly* as expected. If we bear this in mind when on service we shall be prepared for some of the unpleasant surprises which are always happening in war.[5]

Burnside had other options to at least carefully consider. Parts of the Rappahannock River are fordable, even with the river somewhat swollen. Joseph Hooker suggested on November 19 that Burnside move a force upriver and cross to the Fredericksburg side. Burnside said no. Another source of historical debate since that time was whether Burnside should have acted. Detaching some units from easy support by the rest of the army was always risky against a commander as naturally aggressive as Robert E. Lee. Burnside, in his defense, also expected the pontoons to arrive within a day or two.

The pontoons did not arrive until November 24, 1862. Waiting for the pontoons gave Lee time to arrive in strength at Fredericksburg, particularly Marye's Heights, just behind the town. On November 19, Lee had started moving his men toward Fredericksburg. Virtually all his army was in place by November 24, just when the Federal pontoons arrived. Burnside, his hopes for surprise gone, had to find another plan. The best plan he could come up with was a direct assault on Lee's army, on a plain below Fredericksburg and on the heights behind the town. Even this was not a bad plan, if proper focus was put on the plain, and the assault on the heights was just designed to hold the defenders in place.

The first combat elements of the Army of the Potomac crossed on December 11, 1862, after engineers had crossed and built bridges under fire. The bulk of the army crossed the next day. Burnside's men did not attack that day, though Jackson's corps was not fully in position in the south of town.

December 13 saw Federal attacks on Lee's right flank, under Stonewall Jackson, on a plain south of town. The Federal attacks were out of sync here, with insufficient forces being committed to any one area. Federal attacks went directly at Jackson's line, rather than, as Burnside had wanted, going around Jackson's right flank. Some local Federal success, a breakthrough at a portion of Jackson's line, by a division under George Meade, was not followed up, though Meade had urgently requested support.

Operational and tactical coordination was, and would remain, a problem with the Army of the Potomac. Communications of the day made it hard for the commander to get "real time" information on a battle outside his range of vision and communicate instructions. The need for ranking subordinates who understood (even anticipated) and were able and willing to carry out the "commander's intent" was important. But the commander also had the responsibility to keep up to date on his battle, and to ensure that his wishes were being carried out or that subordinates were reacting appropriately to unanticipated changes. Up to this point Lee had such subordinates in Jackson and Longstreet. Whatever their own problems and faults as commanders, McClellan and Burnside did not have such senior subordinates.

The main Federal effort of the day, supposed to be carried out as simultaneously with the attack on the Confederate right, started late and ended up going directly at Lee's left, under James Longstreet, entrenched on and in front of Marye's Heights, just west of town. Burnside called for a tactically simplistic frontal assault—uphill, against the heights and a deadly stone wall just in front of the heights. Divisions attacked individually, though a coordinated attack probably would not have worked. Federal troops did not even reach the wall.

Burnside was talked out of renewing the attack the next day. On December 15, the Federals withdrew back across the river.

Lincoln issued a statement to the Army of the Potomac, a few days after their defeat. "The courage which you, in an open field, maintained the contest against an entrenched foe . . . [shows] that you possess all the qualities of a great army, which will yet give victory to the cause of country and of popular government."[6]

Not long after the Battle of Fredericksburg, meditating on the horrible casualties, the "awful arithmetic," Lincoln realized something else. He told William Stoddard, a junior assistant, "that if the same battle were to be fought over again, every day, through a week of days, with the same relative results, the army under Lee would be wiped out to its last man, the Army of the Potomac would still be a mighty host, the Confederacy gone."[7] (Historian Geoffrey Perret thinks that though Lincoln might have said something like this, it was probably said after the Battle of Chancellorsville.[8])

Burnside quickly began to consider further attacks, thinking about a flanking move west along the Rappahannock River. Meanwhile, on December 30, an extraordinary meeting took place at the White House. Abraham Lincoln met with Brigadier General John Newton, a division commander, and one of Newton's brigade commanders, Brigadier General John Cochrane. They were representing other generals in the army, including a corps commander, William Smith, and a "grand division" commander, William Franklin. Interestingly, despite a reputation as a man quite ready to badmouth, even backstab, his superiors, Joseph Hooker was not among the "conspiring" generals.

Though they claimed they were just expressing concern about the state of the army and Burnside's planned campaign, Cochrane and Newton were at the White House to convince Lincoln that Burnside had to be fired for the good of the army. Lincoln quickly realized what they were doing, but he remained noncommittal. The one immediate result of the meeting was that Lincoln telegraphed Burnside not to make any moves without consulting him first.

However inappropriate the generals' actions, they were on the mark about the poor state of the Army of the Potomac that winter. According to a recent historian,

> At no other point in the war was the Army of the Potomac so dangerously low in spirit and morale as in the winter of 1862–63. Not only had the men lost all confidence in their commanding general, they had no confidence that the high command even knew what it was doing. All the essential ties that bound the army together were unraveling. Each two or three days the equivalent of a regiment deserted and went home.[9]

A significant aside from the history of the Army of the Potomac occurred when the formal Emancipation Proclamation was issued January 1, 1863, as Lincoln had promised just after the Battle of Antietam.

Burnside, during this period, received several statements of support from Lincoln and Halleck.

On January 19, 1863, the Army of the Potomac moved out of its camps and headed west, along the Rappahannock River. It also began to rain. The roads became virtually impassable. By January 22, the infamous "Mud March," a source of great entertainment to the watching Confederates across the river, had ended. Burnside's army slogged back to camp.

On January 23, 1863, Burnside issued General Order No. 8, removing Hooker, Franklin, Smith, and several other generals from the army. The next day he gave Lincoln a choice: endorse the order or accept Burnside's resignation. On January 25, Franklin and Smith were relieved from the Army of the Potomac. Burnside's resignation as commander was accepted. He was persuaded not to resign from the military altogether, but to take leave and await further assignment.

That same day Joseph Hooker was appointed to command the Army of the Potomac. The next day, Hooker received a famous letter from Abraham Lincoln.

> General: I have placed you at the head of the Army of the Potomac. Of course, I have done this upon what appear to me to be sufficient reasons, and yet I

think it is best for you to know that there are some things in regard to which I am not quite satisfied with you. I believe you to be a brave and skillful soldier, which of course I like. I also believe you do not mix politics with your profession, in which you are right. You have confidence in yourself, which is a valuable if not an indispensable quality. You are ambitious, which, within reasonable bounds, does good rather than harm; but I think that during General Burnside's command of the army you have taken counsel of your ambition and thwarted him as much as you could, in which you did a great wrong to the country and to a most meritorious and honorable brother officer. I have heard, in such a way as to believe it, of your recently saying that both the army and the government needed a dictator. Of course it was not for this, but in spite of it, that I have given you the command. Only those generals who gain successes can set up dictators. What I now ask of you is military success, and I will risk the dictatorship. The government will support you to the utmost of its ability, which is neither more nor less than it has done and will do for all commanders. I much fear that the spirit which you have aided to infuse into the army, of criticizing their commander and withholding confidence from him, will now turn upon you. I shall assist you as far as I can to put it down. Neither you nor Napoleon, if he were alive again, could get any good out of an army while such a spirit prevails in it; and now beware of rashness. Beware of rashness, but with energy and sleepless vigilance go forward and give us victories.[10]

Hooker began a series of changes in the way the army was run. Two months after Hooker took over, a soldier from Pennsylvania wrote his sister, "I am well and expect to be in Richmond soon if Joe Hooker leads the way and don't stick in the mud . . . I am in hopes that we shall make Richmond howl this time."[11]

At the time the Pennsylvania soldier's letter was written, the state of the Army of the Potomac was substantially improved from when Hooker had taken over. Practical conditions were improved. Politics among the high command had declined—Hooker seemed to have listened to at least part of Lincoln's advice. Morale of the men had improved substantially.

Hooker began his period in command by eliminating Burnside's structure of three "grand divisions," returning to direct command of eight army corps. Hooker saw the grand division command system as cumbersome, which it could be, as it added an extra step between the commander and his fighting units. However, much of this problem might have come from the men in charge of the grand divisions. Franklin and Edwin Sumner were now out of the army. Hooker, himself, had commanded the third grand division. At least one analyst has pointed out that the most effective Eastern army commanders, Lee in 1862 through 1863 and Meade in 1863 through 1865, worked directly with four "units of maneuver" at the most.[12] Hooker coupled this with dispersing his artillery to division level, lessening central control on the grounds of improving cohesion between artillery and the infantry it was supporting.

Hooker's other reforms were less debatable. He cleared up problems with pay. He improved delivery of fresh food, though partially counterbalancing this by coming up with the idea of mule trains in the immediate area of the front. Mules alone make less noise than wagons, but they can be hard to handle and carried fewer supplies per animal. Hooker unified the cavalry, in theory improving the value of this arm.

Hooker worked to solve the major problem of desertion. He increased patrols to catch deserters. He ordered a system of inspection of packages from home, to ensure families were not sending civilian clothes to aid soldiers in deserting. Hooker persuaded Lincoln to issue a proclamation of amnesty for all deserters who returned to the ranks. Hooker instituted a system of furloughs. He also instituted a system of badges, worn on the uniform, to identify corps and divisions. This made it easy to identify the unit of a straggler and find the officer responsible. It also promoted unit pride. A variation on this system is still used in the modern military.

Hooker appointed Jonathan Letterman as medical director. Letterman instituted a series of sanitation and health improvements. Letterman was the one who arranged for fresher food, including baking bread within the army camps. Letterman cleaned up the camps—including improving placement of latrines as far as possible from living areas and fresh water supplies. In early April Letterman had Hooker order all soldiers to wash themselves and their clothes. Those who did not do so would be arrested. One New York artilleryman wrote home, "General Hooker is bound to have this army start forth in good style with clean clothes, at least."[13]

Appropriately, considering Hooker's reputation as a heavy drinker, he arranged for regiments returning from picket duty to receive a ration of whisky.

One of Hooker's security measures had a lasting impact on American culture. Hooker grew tired of having his plans speculated on, and perhaps given away, in the Northern press. He decided one way to increase press responsibility was to require reporters to sign their pieces when published. Most reports had been published unsigned. Joseph Hooker thus created the modern newspaper "byline."[14]

Hooker had a far better tool than he had inherited from Burnside. He now had to use the tool.

5

CHANCELLORSVILLE

On the whole I think this plan was decidedly the best strategy conceived in any of the campaigns ever set on foot against us.

—Edward Porter Alexander, 1905[1]

Washington, D.C., had a snowstorm on Saturday, April 4, 1863. This rarely happened, though the area has been known to have occasional major snowstorms in March. If this writer's own experience as a long-term resident of the D.C. area is any reflection, even if the storm produced not more than a few inches of snow, it was beautiful when coming down, an epic traffic hassle when finished. Apparently this was a large storm, very windy, with the snow blowing in all directions. Normally this would be of little interest.

This storm made the history books because President Abraham Lincoln was traveling down to Falmouth, Virginia, just across the river from Fredericksburg, to meet with Joseph Hooker and to inspect the Army of the Potomac. When George McClellan commanded the Army of the Potomac, he always seemed to consider discussing his plans with Lincoln, his boss, about on a level with discussing them with the Confederates—communicating with the enemy. Hooker was more communicative, in this respect, at least, being more perceptive than McClellan and recognizing the need to keep the civilian command structure informed of what was going on with its primary army.

Hooker invited Lincoln to come down for talks. Lincoln decided to make a family trip of it, inviting his wife, his son Thomas (called Tad), and several others, including Attorney General Edward Bates. April 4, in fact, was Tad's tenth birthday.

When Lincoln and his party left, it was still snowing heavily. They intended to take a steamer down the Potomac, catching a train at Aquia Creek to Falmouth. They should have reached Falmouth that evening, but the storm made it necessary to take shelter in a cove. Noah Brooks, a journalist accompanying the president, noted that every traveler took shelter below decks from the storm, except for Tad. Tad was determined to catch fish for dinner. He actually did catch one small fish, and was very pleased when it was cooked and served.

Brooks wrote, showing the difference between life then (even during a war) and life today, that no one stood watch on the deck. "It was a rare chance for a daring rebel raid upon our little steamer had the enemy only known that the President of the United States, unattended by any escort and unarmed, was on board the *Carrie Martin*, which peacefully [sat] at anchor all night on the lonely roadstead."[2] Brooks also noted the simplicity of the Lincoln traveling party. It appeared that this was a man out for a relaxing trip with his family. Brooks finished his description by pointing out that nothing history making happened that night.

The snow was still falling when Lincoln and his traveling party arrived at the Federal base at Aquia Creek the next morning. Brooks wrote that the small landing on the Potomac had become a large depot, with huge warehouses and a well-built temporary railroad to take them to the Army of the Potomac headquarters. He provided an example of the size of the operation by pointing out that one million pounds of forage were transported each day to feed the sixty thousand horses and mules with the army. Interestingly, though Brooks mentions the weather—chilly and overcast, but with the snow having stopped—he does not mention how long it took the Lincoln party to get to the end of the line, Falmouth Station, five miles from Hooker's headquarters at Falmouth.

Arriving at Hooker's headquarters, after a carriage ride over muddy roads, the party found that "General Hooker's headquarters are quite as simple and unpretending as any of his men, as he abhors houses and prefers tent life, being unwilling, he says, to live in better quarters than his humblest soldier."[3] There is no indication as to whether this accurately reflected Hooker's views, or whether, not unlikely, he was trying to visibly differentiate himself from McClellan.

Lincoln always found it a refreshing change from Washington to visit the Army of the Potomac. This trip was no exception. Lincoln was encouraged in thinking that Hooker was a more active general and less of a whining and complaining prima donna than McClellan, at least so far. (Lincoln certainly would have considered Hooker a more competent commander than Burnside.) At the end of their meetings, however, Lincoln did warn Hooker and his second in command, Darius Couch, "I want to impress upon you two gentlemen in your next fight . . . put in all of your men."[4] Lincoln had learned from the experience of McClellan possibly missing a chance to win a smashing victory at Antietam by attacking piecemeal, and keeping some twenty thousand men out of the fight.

Attorney General Bates wrote a friend of his, soon after returning to Washington, that "the only cheering thing I have seen this half year is Hooker's army. He has renewed it, in courage, strength, spirit, confidence. He told me with emphasis that he had as many men as he wanted, & as good men."[5] Bates presumably recognized the contrast between Hooker saying he had enough men and McClellan's habit of always asking for reinforcements. Bates had no doubt that Hooker would use the army as well as he had reformed the army.

Joseph Hooker had a far better tool than he had inherited from Burnside. He now had to use the tool. Unlike McClellan, Hooker appeared willing to fight. He now had to show if he could successfully use his tool against his very formidable opponent.

When Hooker began to plan his spring campaign against Lee, in March and April of 1863, the context in which he operated, the situation for the North, was mixed, but hopeful. Ulysses S. Grant and William Sherman were steadily moving on Vicksburg, the more important of two Southern positions remaining on the Mississippi River. The direct approach to Vicksburg from the north had failed. Grant, therefore, marched his army down the west side of the river, crossed to the east bank, on which Vicksburg was located, and then swung around in a broad move to come upon Vicksburg from the land. At the time Hooker was planning his spring campaign, Grant was in the process of winning five battles over two weeks, while suffering far fewer Federal than Confederate casualties.

A second major Federal army, the Army of the Cumberland, under William S. Rosecrans, was in Tennessee getting ready to head East in its spring campaign.

Grant and Rosecrans would try to continue the relatively successful Federal efforts in the Western theater. Hooker, on the other hand, had the task of ending a year-long period of almost unbroken Federal failure in the East—ever since Robert E. Lee took command of the Army of Northern Virginia.

Hooker brought some noticeable personality traits to his command of the Army of the Potomac, as he showed when he announced, "My plans are perfect, and when I start to carry them out, may God have mercy on General Lee, for I will have none."[6] Hooker was not a modest man. But this was the era of generals who were not modest, and all too often Northern generals' ability to produce was in inverse proportion to their modesty. Burnside was the unfortunate exception, not in ability but in modesty. Hooker, as Lincoln pointed out, also had the reputation of a schemer, one who did not just complain but seemed to actively work against his superiors.

So far, however, to use a modern phrase, Hooker talked the talk but he also walked the walk. He had been an excellent division and corps commander. His nickname of "Fighting Joe Hooker," which he did not like, was created by a typographical error. A newspaper headline dropped the dash from "Still Fighting—Joe Hooker."

Hooker brought another interesting characteristic to the table. Hooker, forty-eight at the time of the Battle of Chancellorsville, had graduated West Point with the class of 1837, ranking somewhat below the middle of his class. After service in the Mexican War, in 1853 he resigned his commission, a not uncommon practice. McClellan, Burnside, Grant, and Sherman had done the same, as had Stonewall Jackson.

Hooker had been a gambler before the war, literarily, with poker. Within limits, gambling is a useful trait for a commander, the willingness to take carefully considered risks for potentially great gain. During the Mexican War, and the years after, as one recent historian has written, "By diligent practice he developed a reputation as one of the sharpest poker players in the army, noted for his ability to stake all on the turn of a single card."[7]

Hooker's "old army" career took him to California after the Mexican War. It was here that some associates began to notice something about Hooker. Hooker maintained his basic skill in poker, notably his ability to bluff and deceive an opponent. An officer who knew him in the pre–Civil War army, George Stoneman, then a lieutenant, and who commanded Federal cavalry at Chancellorsville, later discussed one particular habit of Hooker the poker player, whom he had observed at length when they served together. Stoneman remarked that Hooker had one problem with his general poker skill. Bluff is a part of poker, convincing the opponent you hold more cards than you actually hold. But, Stoneman remarked, Hooker "could play the best game of poker I ever saw until it came to the point when he should go a thousand better, and then he would flunk."[8] The only indication as to when this conversation took place, and any prejudices Stoneman brought to his statement, was provided by Alexander McClure, the writer and a veteran of the Army of the Potomac: "I dined with General Stoneman in Washington soon after the battle."[9]

Evidence of this bad habit comes in Hooker's accumulation of gambling debts, showing that he seemed to lack the ability, or personality/character, for playing constant winning poker. Hooker did manage to keep ahead of his debts after his 1853 resignation from the army. Though not particularly successful in his efforts at farming and other careers, Hooker avoided disaster. (There is no indication as to how well Hooker did in poker between 1853 and the start of the war.) Like Grant, Hooker seemed to have found his niche when the Civil War broke out in 1861.

Hooker started well against Robert E. Lee. Hooker's plans for the May 1863 operations were good, though probably not as good as when Hooker declared: "My plans are perfect, and when I start to carry them out, may God have mercy on General Lee, for I will have none."[10]

Part of Hooker's army, the VI Corps and some other units, all under the command of John Sedgwick, would create a diversion at Fredericksburg. Sedgwick's job was to make Lee think the main Federal attack was coming at Fredericksburg.

The bulk of the army would swing around Lee's left flank, through the heavily wooded area known as the Wilderness, lure Lee out of his fortifications near Fredericksburg, and then destroy him in open battle or force him back to the Richmond defenses for a siege, which the North was likely to eventually win. One Confederate officer later wrote, "On the whole I think this plan was decidedly the best strategy conceived in any of the campaigns ever set on foot against us."[11]

Hooker recognized that Lee was likely to have some idea that the Federals were moving around his left. If he thought Sedgwick's effort was a diversion, Lee would send his men after Hooker's main force. Sedgwick was given the task of fooling one of the most astute military minds of the period. In creating his diversion, Sedgwick had to balance creating believability with the fact that it was a diversion, a secondary effort where he should not risk high casualties.

Hooker's immediate need for the diversion was while his flanking column was crossing the Rapidan River, when it was most vulnerable. His goal for Sedgwick and the Confederates, he wrote Lincoln, was to keep the Southern soldiers "in their places, and if they should detach heavy forces to attack the troops coming down the river; to storm and carry those works and take possession of the enemy's short line of retreat."[12]

All commanders need good intelligence of what the enemy is doing. Hooker's plan required him to have a particularly accurate idea of Lee's activities, as close to "real time" intelligence as was possible at the time. Hooker's sources of intelligence would vary during the campaign.

Hooker had developed an excellent military intelligence service, with knowledgeable sources behind Confederate lines. One member, a sergeant recruited from an Indiana cavalry unit, managed to tour the entire line of Southern encampments behind the Rappahannock River. No one quite knows how he got away with it. Historian Stephen Sears theorizes that he disguised himself as one of John Mosby's rangers,[13] sometimes strange-looking but confident people who seemed to know what they were doing. The result was that most of Lee's major units were identified and located.

A man named Isaac Silver lived in the area, three miles east of the Chancellor House, even then known as Chancellorsville. Silver had been born in the North and remained loyal to the North. A friend of Silver's, with a secret route for crossing the lines, brought Silver's reports. The first report, in March, gave information on Lee's units, down to brigade level. In a major change from McClellan, Hooker was supplied with reasonably accurate reports of Lee's strength.

There would be several problems with Hooker's intelligence efforts. The Federals had what might be called aerial reconnaissance, two balloons operated by Thaddeus Sobieski Constantine Lowe, usually called Professor Lowe, though he apparently was not actually a professor. Lowe was first rate as a balloon scientist and technician. For example, he invented a portable hydrogen generator to make it easy to transport the balloons. Unfortunately, he was not a very skilled military observer. He would report such things as a "large force" of enemy, giving no indication of what he considered a large force. (This analysis problem had also surfaced during the Peninsula Campaign.) On one particular report, where Lowe used that term, *large force*, Hooker wrote, "What does the Professor call a large force?"[14] These problems in analysis were partly corrected when army chief engineer Cyrus Comstock, who could better evaluate and give more specifics on enemy strength, began doing some of the observing.

Lowe resigned on April 12, 1863. In addition to being placed under the control of Captain Comstock, Lowe's fee was also lowered. He gave this as his reason for resigning. However, in his resignation letter to Comstock, Lowe wrote, "Notwithstanding, as I have promised the Command'g Gen'l that nothing should be lacking on my part to render the greatest possible service during the next battle, and as I consider that all should be done that genius can devise to make the first move by our Chief Commander successful,

I will offer my services until that time, free of charge to the Gov't."[15] The balloon service would be abolished with Lowe's departure a few days after the end of the Chancellorsville campaign.

Current intelligence, what might be called operational or tactical intelligence, was supplied during the Civil War by cavalry. Unfortunately, Hooker's plan called for the cavalry to leave almost two weeks before the army advanced, on a very wide sweep toward Richmond, designed to cut Lee's supply lines and pull him out of his entrenchments.

Hooker's plan required careful coordination and communication among its various elements, and with its commander. Despite use of the telegraph, communication was always a problem with the technology of the time. The enemy frequently cut telegraph lines. The heavily forested and tangled terrain of the Chancellorsville-Wilderness area created difficulties for couriers in finding various Federal commanders. Hooker would spend time with his maneuver units and away from his headquarters before moving his headquarters closer to the front lines. Normally an admirable command practice, this made it harder to find Hooker to keep him informed of developments and get appropriate instructions. Finally, the Federals were trying a new telegraphic system, which did not always work. One can be too high tech.

Hooker was facing, in Robert E. Lee, an opponent likely to take advantage of any mistakes. A few days after the Battle of Fredericksburg, the *Charleston Mercury* had written, "General Lee knows his business and that army has known no such word as fail."[16] Lee thought the same thing about his army, becoming more and more convinced his army could do whatever he asked—even with part of James Longstreet's First Corps, and Longstreet himself, on detached duty in southeastern Virginia and unlikely to play a role in the spring campaign.

The "action" began on Monday, April 27, 1863, when Hooker's units began to advance. "Warning orders" had gone to Federal corps commanders on Saturday, April 25. On Sunday, part of which the Confederate high command spent in religious services, the Federals were drafting formal orders and getting ready to start the campaign.

Hooker was very security conscious. Lee was a tough enough opponent when he did not know what you were trying to do. Even on Sunday, April 26, Hooker's senior corps commanders only had a vague idea of their movements for the next day.

April 27 and 28 saw Federal forces concentrating and moving northwest along the Rappahannock River. Other forces, under John Sedgwick, made preparations for crossing this river just south of Fredericksburg. Several of

Sedgwick's subordinate generals suggested a real attack in this area. However, this contradicted the letter, if not the spirit, of Sedgwick's orders. Sedgwick was not a man to improvise and launch a real attack.

> Speaking for Hooker, Chief of Staff Dan Butterfield had instructed Sedgwick to Telegraph us freely early in the morning. Keep a good look at the size and number of campfires. It is very important to know whether or not the enemy are being held in your front. The moment news arrives with regard to the progress made to-day by the right wing, plans for to-morrow will issue. The maneuvers now in progress the general hopes will compel the enemy to fight him on his own ground. He has no desire to make the general engagement where you are.[17]

The next day, Sedgwick was given orders that seemed to authorize him to take advantage of any Confederate weakness on his front. "It is not known, of course, what effect the [main Federal] advance will have upon the enemy, and the general commanding directs that you observe his movements with the utmost vigilance, and, should he expose a weak point, attack him in full force and destroy him."[18] It remained to be seen how good a diversion Sedgwick could provide, and if he had the initiative to see when a real attack might work.

Jackson wanted to attack Sedgwick before Sedgwick could attack the Confederates. Fitz Lee described this view in a speech in 1879:

> In a conversation with a Confederate officer at Lexington, on February 16, 1868, General Lee said, in regard to Chancellorsville, that "Jackson at first preferred to attack Sedgwick's force in the plain at Fredericksburg, but he told him he feared it was as impracticable as it was at the first battle of Fredericksburg. It was hard to get at the enemy and harder to get away if we drove him into the river." "But," said he to Jackson: "If you think it can be done, I will give orders for it." Jackson then asked to be allowed to examine the ground, and did so during the afternoon, and at night came to Lee and said he thought he (Lee) was right. "It would be inexpedient to attack there." "Move then," said Lee, "at dawn tomorrow (the 1st May) up to Anderson," who had been previously ordered to proceed towards Chancellorsville; "and the next time I saw Jackson," said General Lee, "was upon the next day, when he was on our skirmish line, driving in the enemy's skirmishers around Chancellorsville."[19]

Sedgwick's diversion did not work. Lee never considered Sedgwick's advance to be Hooker's main effort. Later on April 29 Confederate cavalry detected Federal troops crossing into the Wilderness and sent word to Lee. This focused Lee's attention on the Wilderness and started to confirm Lee's expectations of a Federal flanking effort. Later that day Lee reported to Jefferson Davis:

> The enemy crossed the Rappahannock to-day in large numbers, and have taken position under the bank of the river, under cover of their heavy guns on the opposite side.
>
> The day has been favorable for his operations, and to-night he will probably get over the remainder of his forces.
>
> Besides the force which was reported by General Stuart to have crossed on the pontoon bridges laid below Kelly's Ford, I have learned this evening by couriers from Germanna and Ely's Fords that the enemy's cavalry crossed the Rapidan at those points about 2 p.m. today. I could not learn their strength, but infantry was said to have crossed with the cavalry at the former point.
>
> Their intention, I presume, is to turn our left, and probably to get into our rear. Our scattered condition favors their operations. I hope if any re-enforcements can be sent, they may be forwarded immediately.[20]

There is no indication that Lee was seriously considering retreat, which would provide a practical need to kept bridges to the south open, but he had to take into account all possibilities.

Lee responded to the Federal movements by sending Richard Anderson's division, under Lee's direct command in the absence of Longstreet, to intercept the Federals at the river crossing. After his cavalry informed Lee of the close proximity of stronger Federal forces, Lee ordered Anderson to pull back somewhat. In the hours before midnight, Anderson had his division take position not far from the Chancellor House.

After sunrise on April 30, Anderson was able to get a better look at his division's position. The division was covering the roads Anderson had been ordered to cover. However, due to the thick woods, the division had poor visibility. His men might not be able to see flanking forces. Acting on his own initiative, under Lee's discretionary orders, Anderson withdrew three miles to the east, to a position in the open, and began to entrench.

That afternoon Lee fully realized what Hooker was attempting. He had ridden up to the hill in back of the Confederates lines, now known as Lee's Hill, which he had occupied during most of the Battle of Fredericksburg. He spent a while studying Federal lines through a spyglass, closed the glass, and then remarked to his aide Charles Marshall, "The main attack will come from above."[21]

Rather than panicking, or freezing into inaction, Lee then risked the "classic error" of splitting his army with an enemy nearby. After Jackson told Lee he no longer thought an attack on Sedgwick feasible, Lee began to move Jackson's Second Corps divisions to intercept Hooker. Jubal Early was left with his own division, and some additional units, to hold Fredericksburg against vastly superior Federal forces on that front. Lee could see that the Federals were not moving very quickly in the immediate Fredericksburg front, and knew the Marye's Heights position in back of the town was as strong as it had been the December before, though less well manned, but this was still a risk.

About noon that day, the Federal V Corps, under George Meade, began to arrive in the area of the Chancellor House, the planned Federal concentration point. A few hours later, talking with General Henry Slocum, commander of the XII Corps, Meade expressed pleasure at how well the advance had gone. He proposed to Slocum that they continue the march, and get out of the Wilderness as soon as possible. Meade was clearly disappointed when Slocum said Hooker had ordered them to stay where they were, to await the arrival of the II and III Corps. Meade even had to recall one of his units that had already pushed ahead and spotted entrenched Confederates.

Fighting Robert E. Lee, one always expected surprises. Hooker wanted to stick with a plan that appeared to be working. A military truism is that plans fall apart at first contact with the enemy. But plans can fall apart positively as well as negatively. Unexpected opportunities as well as unexpected problems can arise, and a good commander has to be willing and able to take advantage. Hooker, however, was ten miles from Meade and Slocum, having returned to headquarters across the Rappahannock at Falmouth. Deteriorating Federal communications handicapped him, and he might not have realized how well his plan was working. Of course, as the poker example discussed earlier shows, Hooker might also have started to lose confidence, just when the time came to go one bluff better than your opponent, particularly when you had the power to back up the bluff.

Hooker's last major action the evening of April 30 was to issue his ironically phrased order to his army, summarizing progress so far:

> It is with heartfelt satisfaction the commanding general announces to the army that the operations of the last three days have determined that our enemy must either ingloriously fly, or come out from behind his defenses and give us battle on our own ground.[22]

There is no way to know if Hooker ever heard the old saying, "Be careful what you ask for, you might get it."

May 1, 1863, is considered the start of the "formal" Battle of Chancellorsville. Early that morning, the uncertainly reliable Federal balloon observers reported that Jackson's corps was still in the Fredericksburg area, facing Sedgwick. Jackson was already on his way to the Wilderness. Most of the Federal cavalry, which might have detected Jackson's move, was too far away on Hooker's wide sweep in the general direction of Richmond to play any part in the forthcoming battle. Hooker had lost his previous intelligence advantage over Lee.

Hooker ordered an advance that morning on the "Chancellorsville front." George Sykes led his V Corps division east along the Orange Turnpike. Other Federal units advanced along the Orange Plank Road to the south and the River Road to the north. At about this same time, Jackson ordered his men to advance west on the two roads to the south of the Orange turnpike.

George Meade's V Corps met virtually no resistance on the River Road. The lead Federal elements on the Orange Turnpike made contact with the Confederates, and fighting started about 11:30 a.m. The situation on the parallel Orange Plank Road was more unusual. The Confederates on this road actually advanced past the Federal forces on the Turnpike. In the thick woods, neither side was aware of the enemy on their right flank. Environment can sometimes actively work against a commander.

Not that there are good places to fight battles, but the Wilderness was a particularly bad place to fight a battle. The view down the arms of the Orange Plank Road/Brock Road crossroads, in any direction, even today is fifty to seventy-five yards at most, less than the effective range of a Civil War musket or rifle. The unobstructed view in the woods, off the road, is measured in feet, and not many of them. Trees sometimes block the sun, making it hard to tell direction. At the time of the battle, the woods were thicker, more tangled, and more widespread than they are today. The smoke from black powder weapons would have limited even more a soldier's range of vision.

One writer later described the general area:

> It is impossible to conceive a field worse adapted to the movements of a grand army. The whole face of the country is thickly wooded, with only an occasional opening, and intersected by a few narrow wood-roads. But the woods of the wilderness have not the ordinary features of a forest. The region rests on a belt of mineral rocks, and for above a hundred years, extensive mining has been carried on. To feed the mines the timber of the country for many miles around had been cut down, and in its place there had arisen a dense undergrowth. . . . It is a region of gloom and the shadow of death. Maneuvering here was necessarily out of the question, and only Indian tactics told. The troops could

only receive direction by the point of the compass; for not only were the lines of battle entirely hidden from the sight of the commander, but no officer could see ten files on each side of him. Artillery was wholly ruled out of use; the massive concentrations of three hundred guns stood silent, and only an occasional piece or section could be brought into play on the roadsides. Cavalry was still more useless.[23]

Enemy bullets would come terrifyingly out of the mist, and soldiers would have to shoot into the mist at targets they could not see. Clearings would not have come as a relief. Soldiers only made better targets.

Commanders could not properly direct or control their men, which made the Battle of Chancellorsville, and the Battle of the Wilderness a year later, more a series of small engagements than a major battle. An officer in a New York regiment later described what combat in the forest was like for him: "We could not advance in company front. It was even difficult for a single man to move ahead in the thicket. We broke into columns marching by fours; even then we could not keep that formation. Then we went on as best we could in single file, breaking our way through the pine branches."[24]

The battle that May 1 flowed back and forth for several hours. Union troops were pushed back on the Orange Turnpike by Confederate reinforcements, putting this Confederate advance actually behind Federal lines advancing on two parallel roads. In the dense woods, neither side knew what was happening just a few hundred yards away. The battle as a whole was still an open question. Hooker, however, ordered his men to withdraw to their positions of the previous evening. His corps commanders were surprised, feeling that Hooker was giving up a fight that could have been won. George Meade, for example, is reported as having said, "If he can't hold the top of the hill, how does he expect to hold the bottom?"[25] Why Hooker not only stopped his advance but pulled back his troops on April 30, and again on May 1, became a major question not only for historians but also for observers at the time. The April 30 halt might be explained as a result of poor communications between Hooker and his corps commanders leading the advance. Hooker might have felt the desire not to improvise with a plan that seemed to be working. In the spring of 1863 one would be hard-pressed to fault a commander for not wanting to overreach against Lee and Jackson.

By May 1 Hooker was on the scene at the Chancellor House. Lee's reputation, a "force multiplier" in itself, was now in play. Federal commanders always seemed to inflate the size of Lee's force, inflate even his considerable ability and what he might do with his army. Hooker was losing his confidence that only God would have mercy on Lee, and that Hooker's plans were perfect. More days of battle would follow, and Hooker would have to make more decisions, but he had already made one potentially fatal error. He was not only losing confidence, finding himself unable to play the final card, but also Hooker had let the initiative pass to Lee and Jackson.

Lee and Jackson were already noted as both smart and fierce opponents, quite willing to adopt unconventional strategy if they thought it would work. James Power Smith, one of Jackson's aides, later paraphrased Jackson himself and explained that Jackson "mystified and deceived the enemy."[26] Smith also wrote, "Outwardly, Jackson was not a stone wall, for it was not in his nature to be stable and defensive, but vigorously active. He was an avalanche from an unexpected quarter. He was a thunderbolt from a clear sky. And yet he was in character and will more like a stone wall than any man I have known."[27]

A West Point classmate later wrote, "His chief characteristics as a military leader were his quick perceptions of the weak points of the enemy, his ever readiness, the astounding rapidity of his movements, his sudden and unexpected onslaughts, and the persistency with which he followed them up."[28]

That evening, Lee and Jackson were surprised at Hooker's breaking off his attack and pulling back his forces. Only one of Hooker's three columns had been heavily pressed. Federal commanders at the time, in the same position, would have sat and worried. Lee and Jackson were more concerned with finding a way to attack Hooker's forces.

While Lee and Jackson were discussing attack options, including a flank attack, cavalry leader Jeb Stuart arrived with a report on Federal positions. The Federal far right flank, Oliver Otis Howard's XI Corps, was "in the air," not properly defended or anchored on a natural obstacle. Despite common belief that it was Jackson, Lee was the one who proposed a wide flanking movement around the Federal right—though Jackson quickly agreed. Jackson proposed taking his entire corps of just under thirty thousand men, leaving Lee with only thirteen thousand men to hold off Hooker's seventy-five thousand men nearby.

Jackson's route the next day was not entirely hidden from Federal views. This actually proved an advantage for the Confederates. With the exception of one attack on Jackson's column, which accomplished little, senior Federal commanders were not taking active measures to determine enemy intentions. This is one role of cavalry: to go out and make contact with the enemy and try to determine what the enemy is doing. The overwhelming bulk of the Federal cavalry, however, was not there.

When the Federals saw Jackson's men seemingly headed south, they thought this must mean that Lee was withdrawing. This fit with Hooker's declaration that Lee would have to fight or flee. Humans have an unfortunate tendency to fit new facts into already established interpretations—to let facts fit the conclusions, or at least what one thinks is the proper conclusion. One might even say that people are more willing to lie to themselves than to lie to others.

However, even with the Confederates' apparent southward movement, Hooker should not have assumed Lee was retreating. Commanders should take their own conventional wisdoms into account, and realize they might be wrong. Besides, another fact Hooker had available, which he should have considered, was that retreating without fighting was very much out of character for Lee.

The leading elements of Jackson's corps reached the point where they were to turn north about 2 p.m. Brigadier General Fitz Lee, a Southern cavalry commander and Robert E. Lee's nephew, told Jackson there was a place where he could get a safe view of the Federal right flank. Fitz Lee later spoke about this in a speech after the war:

Jackson was marching on. My cavalry was well in his front. Upon reaching the Plank road, some five miles west of Chancellorsville, my command was halted, and while waiting for Jackson to come up, I made a personal reconnoissance [*sic*] to locate the Federal right for Jackson's attack. With one staff officer, I rode across and beyond the Plank road, in the direction of the Old turnpike, pursuing a path through the woods, momentarily expecting to find evidence of the enemy's presence. Seeing a wooded hill in the distance, I determined, if possible, to get upon its top, as it promised a view of the adjacent country. Cautiously I ascended its side, reaching the open spot upon its summit without molestation. What a sight presented itself before me! Below, and but a few hundred yards distant, ran the Federal line of battle. I was in rear of Howard's right. There were the line of defence, with abatis in front, and long lines of stacked arms in rear. Two cannon were visible in the part of the line seen. The soldiers were in groups in the rear, laughing, chatting, smoking, probably engaged, here and there, in games of cards, and other amusements indulged in while feeling safe and comfortable, awaiting orders. In rear of them were other parties driving up and butchering beeves. The remembrance of the scene is as clear as it was sixteen years ago. So impressed was I with my discovery, that I rode rapidly back to the point on the Plank road where I had left my cavalry, and back down the road Jackson was moving, until I met "Stonewall" himself. "General," said I, "if you will ride with me, halting your column here, out of sight, I will show you the enemy's right, and you will perceive the great advantage of attacking down the Old turnpike instead of the Plank road, the enemy's lines being taken in reverse. Bring only one courier, as you will be in view from the top of the hill." Jackson assented, and I rapidly conducted him to the point of observation. There had been no change in the picture.

I only knew Jackson slightly. I watched him closely as he gazed upon Howard's troops. It was then about 2 P.M. His eyes burned with a brilliant glow, lighting up a sad face. His expression was one of intense interest, his face was colored slightly with the paint of approaching battle, and radiant at the success of his flank movement. . . . To the remarks made to him while the unconscious line of blue was pointed out, he did not reply once during the five minutes he was on the hill, and yet his lips were moving. From what I have read and heard of Jackson since that day, I know now what he was doing then. Oh! "beware of rashness," General Hooker. Stonewall Jackson is praying in full view and in rear of your right flank! While talking to the Great God of Battles, how could he hear what a poor cavalryman was saying. "Tell General Rodes," said he, suddenly whirling his horse towards the courier, "to move across the Old plank road; halt when he gets to the Old turnpike, and I will join him there."[29]

By 5 p.m. the Confederates were in position. Jackson looked around at a group of officers, and saw that most had been either professors or students at the Virginia Military Institute, where Jackson had taught before the Civil War started. He remarked, "The Institute will be heard from today."[30] He then gave the orders to advance on an unsuspecting Federal XI Corps.

The XI Corps, under Oliver Otis Howard, was on the far right of Hooker's line. Though the flank tends to be the most vulnerable part of an army's defense position, and an inviting target of attack, placement in this position was not meant as a compliment to Howard or to his corps.

The XI Corps had come under Howard's command as a way to solve several problems. The men of the corps had been under the command of Major General Franz Sigel, a politically important German immigrant leader, in the Shenandoah Valley. Sigel's little army was among those Federal forces Jackson defeated in his Valley Campaign. After the Battle of Fredericksburg Sigel created a problem. Hooker had commanded one of the grand divisions. Sigel commanded another. With the grand divisions being abolished, Sigel faced becoming just a corps commander, and of the smallest corps in the army. Sigel, ignoring his poor combat record, felt that as senior major general in the Army of the Potomac, outranking even Hooker, he deserved a larger command. Sigel resigned when Lincoln said it was the largest command he could have.

Sigel had been very popular with the Germans and the others in his corps. Though making up probably less than half the strength of the corps, German immigrants and German Americans gave the corps its identity. Hooker did not think that the command should be given to Carl Schurz, senior division commander and another prominent German immigrant. Hooker was not convinced Schurz could run the corps effectively.

Hooker also had another problem with a general demanding a post appropriate to his seniority. Daniel Sickles, another important political general, was appointed to head the III Corps. Howard, a division commander in the II Corps, complained that he was senior to Sickles. Hooker, to quiet Howard and to keep from having to give the command to Schurz, gave it to Howard. This was not popular with the men of the corps. Howard's "time" would come at Chancellorsville. Sickles had to wait until Gettysburg to show what he could do.

Hooker expected the primary routes of Confederate attack to be west along the River Road and the Orange Road. Both roads were covered by George Meade's V Corps and Henry Slocum's XII Corps, both far better in Hooker's estimation than Howard's men. Howard and his corps were placed as far away from the expected action as possible.

Hooker began to have second thoughts about the location of the likely Confederate attack. He even warned Howard to pay attention to his right, and be sure it was not vulnerable to a flank attack. But Howard took no action, and Hooker did not check to see whether Howard had taken action. Hooker did order John Reynolds to take the Federal I Corps into position on the right. But this order was given too late, and it arrived even later. Reynolds did not make it on time.

The first signs the Union forces of Howard's corps on the right had of the Confederate attack late that afternoon were terrified animals crashing out of the woods. The Federal troops had just a moment or two to laugh until thousands of Confederate troops followed the animals. The Federal right crumbled. Darius Couch later wrote:

> It was about 5:30 in the evening when the head of Jackson's column found itself on the right and rear of the army, which on that flank consisted of the Eleventh Corps, the extreme right brigade receiving its first intimation of danger from a volley of musketry fired into their rear, followed up so impetuously that no efficient stand could be made by the brigades of the corps that successively attempted to resist the enemy's charge. . . . I suspect that the prime reason for the surprise was that the superior officers of the right corps had been put off their guard by adopting the conjecture of Hooker, "Lee's army is in full retreat to Gordonsville," as well as expecting the enemy to attack precisely where ample preparations had been made to receive him. It can be emphatically stated that no corps in the army, surprised as the Eleventh was at this time, could have held its ground under similar circumstances.[31]

A staff officer from the XI Corps, some years after the war, blamed the disaster on the XI's corps commander and divisional commanders. The officer wrote, "The findings of this inquiry show, or seem to show, that warnings of the massing of the enemy's forces on the flank and rear of the Eleventh Corps were sent at different times to the headquarters of the First Division and to the corps, but we have not found any evidence that they were forwarded to army headquarters. . . . Neither do we find any evidence to show that either Devens, Howard, or Hooker took any measures after midday to ascertain if the right flank of the Army of the Potomac was free from danger."[32]

The officer wrote about the men of the corps that "the investigation clearly proves that the disastrous results of the battle of Chancellorsville cannot be justly ascribed to the want of vigilance and soldierly conduct on the part of the rank and file of the Eleventh Corps."[33] In other words, this officer agreed with Couch—don't blame the men.

Darkness, and Federal troops alerted by the noise and given time to prepare, eventually halted the Confederates. The Confederates paid a heavy cost for success that evening. Stonewall Jackson was riding in front of his lines, scouting for a new attack, when his own men accidentally and seriously wounded him. Jackson turned over command to his senior division commander, A. P. Hill. When Hill himself was wounded a few moments later, cavalry commander James Ewell Brown "Jeb" Stuart was given temporary command of the corps.

The most surprising aspect of the Battle of Chancellorsville is that its most famous incident, Jackson's flank attack, did not decide the battle. The Federals had suffered a major reverse on their right but had still not irredeemably lost. The Federals were actually forced back to a stronger and more compact position than before Jackson's attack.

Unfortunately for Federal morale, particularly that of Hooker, the one who counted most, Lee and Jackson had pulled off exactly the type of surprise the Federals had feared. This should be the reason that Jackson's attack is considered key to the results at Chancellorsville. General Couch overstated things only slightly when he later wrote:

> The situation of Jackson's corps on the morning of May 3d was a desperate one, its front and right flank being in the presence of not far from 25,000 men, with its left flank subject to an assault of 30,000, the corps of Meade and Reynolds, by advancing them to the right, where the thicket did not present an insurmountable obstacle. It only required that Hooker should brace himself up to take a common-sense view of the state of things, when the success gained

by Jackson would have turned into an overwhelming defeat. But Hooker had become very despondent. I think that his being outgeneraled by Lee had a good deal to do with his depression.[34]

In heavy fighting on May 3, the Army of the Potomac was driven out of the important position of Hazel Grove. The major artillery position of Fairview soon became untenable. Fairview, and Chancellorsville itself (Chancellorsville was actually just a residence), had to be evacuated. The battle was close, though, and had Hooker chosen to commit all his men, it might still have turned into a victory for the Federals, or at least an Antietam-style tactical stalemate.

A significant event that morning, about 9:30 a.m., was that a shell injured Hooker himself. The shell hit a pillar of the Chancellorsville house on which Hooker was leaning, throwing part of the pillar into Hooker and then throwing Hooker, hard, to the ground. Hooker's injury, a concussion, probably helped cause the rumor that he was either drunk or had picked the wrong time to "go on the wagon," to stop drinking. Couch may be the one who started that story, writing about twenty years later, "As to the charge that the battle was lost because the general was intoxicated, I have always stated that it would have been far better for him to have continued in his usual habit in that respect. The shock from being violently thrown to the ground, together with the physical exhaustion resulting from loss of sleep and the anxiety of mind incident to the last six days of the campaign, would tell on any man."[35] Symptoms of a head injury can duplicate either being drunk or too suddenly on the wagon. Hooker was also given some brandy, frequently used for medicinal purposes, which also did not help his image.

A greater problem came not from Hooker's being irresponsible but thinking he was being responsible and staying in command. He should have turned over command to his senior subordinate, Darius Couch. Jackson had immediately turned over command to Hill when he was wounded. Daniel Butterfield, as chief of staff, might have given temporary command to Couch. But Butterfield was miles away, back at Falmouth.

With the withdrawal of the Federals to a very strong position anchored on the Rappahannock, the focus of the action of the battle shifted from Hooker and the main Federal force to John Sedgwick and the forces at Fredericksburg.

On May 1, when Robert E. Lee realized Hooker's main attack would be in the Wilderness, he left Jubal Early, with Early's division and some other units, 12,400 men, to hold Sedgwick and 22,500 men in place at Fredericksburg. If the Federals advanced in "overpowering" force, Early was to retreat toward Richmond. If Sedgwick's men recrossed the Rappahannock, Early was to reinforce Lee. On May 2, however, Early received what appeared to be orders from Lee to move immediately to Lee's assistance. Lee's chief of staff, however, had mistransmitted these orders. Lee had actually wanted Early to leave Fredericksburg only if Early detected a weakening of Federal forces on his front. Early left William Barksdale's brigade in place and began moving the rest of his men west. Fortunately for the Confederates, Sedgwick made no move to respond to Early's apparent withdrawal.

Sedgwick finally attacked on the morning of May 3, obeying a direct order from Hooker to do so, making his main assault against Marye's Heights and the Stone Wall—positions infamous from the Battle of Fredericksburg the December before. When he learned of this attack, Early ordered his men to turn back to meet the threat in their rear.

At first, the Federal attacks seemed a replay of the slaughter of the previous December's battle. However, after the second assault, a truce was declared to help the wounded. Federal soldiers noticed the Confederate positions were thinly held, and reported this to their commanders. A third attack was ordered, pressed harder than the first two, and finally took the Confederate positions.

Sedgwick rested his men until 3 p.m. that afternoon—speed rarely being a Federal priority at this point in the war—and then pushed on toward Chancellorsville. Wilcox's Confederate brigade, from Anderson's division, sent from Banks Ford, arrived too late to help Barksdale, but it did its best to delay Sedgwick's advance west. Wilcox's brigade managed to prevent Sedgwick from arriving at Salem Church for almost three hours. Sedgwick finally attacked at 5:30 that evening. He made some progress, though four more brigades had reinforced Wilcox. When Confederate reinforcements arrived at Salem Church, Sedgwick was persuaded to give up the attack. Fighting pretty much ended with darkness that day.

Sedgwick wanted to return to Fredericksburg on May 4, but Early had reoccupied the town. Sedgwick then found himself with a more immediate problem. Lee had split his army again, leaving Stuart with a relatively small force to hold Hooker and the bulk of the Federal army in place while Lee moved to intercept Sedgwick. This was not hard to do. Hooker was in a defensive mood, waiting for Sedgwick to come and rescue him.

Hooker later claimed that the Confederates were so well entrenched that an attack would have failed. Attacking, Hooker commented during his only later visit to the battlefield, in 1876, "would seem to have been the reasonable thing to do. But we were in this impenetrable thicket. All the roads and openings leading through it the enemy immediately fortified strongly, and planted thickly his artillery commanding all the avenues, so that with reduced numbers he could easily hold his lines."[36] One has to imagine Lee or Jackson finding a way to attack under those circumstances. Lee seems to still have been defeating Hooker thirteen years after the battle.

Sedgwick's forces fought off heavy attacks all day on May 4, finally withdrawing to a strong defensive position around Banks's ford, about halfway between Fredericksburg and Hooker's position.

Lee was planning to attack Hooker's main force on May 6, despite the apparent strength of Hooker's defensive position. However, partly covered by rain the night before, Hooker had withdrawn over the river. Hooker held a conference of war, as Couch narrated:

> At 12 o'clock on the night of the 4th–5th General Hooker assembled his corps commanders in council. Meade, Sickles, Howard, Reynolds, and myself were present; General Slocum, on account of the long distance from his post, did not arrive until after the meeting was broken up. Hooker stated that his instructions compelled him to cover Washington, not to jeopardize the army, etc. It was seen by the most casual observer that he had made up his mind to retreat. We were left by ourselves to consult, upon which Sickles made an elaborate argument, sustaining the views of the commanding general. Meade was in favor of fighting, stating that he doubted if we could get off our guns. Howard was in favor of fighting, qualifying his views by the remark that our present situation was due to the bad conduct of his corps, or words to that effect. Reynolds, who was lying on the ground very much fatigued, was in favor of an advance. I had similar views to those of Meade as to getting off the guns, but said I "would favor an advance if I could designate the point of attack." Upon collecting the suffrages, Meade, Reynolds, and Howard voted squarely for an advance, Sickles and myself squarely no; upon which Hooker informed the council that he should take upon himself the responsibility of retiring the army to the other side of the river. As I stepped out of the tent Reynolds, just behind me, broke out, "What was the use of calling us together at this time of night when he intended to retreat anyhow?"[37]

Even his enemy thought Hooker had withdrawn too soon. One Confederate later wrote, after inspecting the Federal defenses a few days later, "I had no idea the enemy was so well fortified and wonder why they left their works so soon."[38] "Had it been Grant in command, he would not have dreamed of giving up the fight,"[39] a second Confederate wrote some years after the war. Hooker, however, had given up the fight, and the Chancellorsville campaign was over.

The ultimate meaning of the Battle of Chancellorsville lies in Hooker's withdrawal back across the Rappahannock River. Eleven days after the start of the campaign, and thirty thousand Federal and Confederate casualties later, both armies were back where they had started. Hooker clearly had done badly at Chancellorsville. Objectively, he lost the battle. However, his decision to withdraw showed not only a loss of confidence but also an exclusive focus on the battle over the campaign. One historian has even recently speculated that had Hooker won at Chancellorsville, he would not have been prepared to successfully follow up the victory.[40]

Lee, at least initially, seemed less than satisfied with his victory at Chancellorsville, seeming to recognize the ultimately inconclusive nature of the result. He was later quoted as having commented in July 1863, to a Confederate government official, that "At Chancellorsville, we gained another victory; our people were wild with delight—I, on the contrary, was more depressed than after Fredericksburg; our loss was severe, and again we had gained not an inch of ground and the enemy could not be pursued."[41]

One particularly severe loss to the Confederacy occurred on May 10, 1863, when Stonewall Jackson died.

Theories abound as to why Hooker lost the battle. His plan was good, but he did not ensure its implementation. The only major planning error was depending too much on careful coordination of different elements of his army. Hooker was pushing the envelope, to use another modern term, of his communications, even had they worked as planned.

A commander can maintain the initiative by forcing the enemy to attack him on grounds of his choosing. The "blocking position" idea can work even today. But Hooker failed to be sure his defensive positions were strong enough and flexible enough to resist whatever nasty surprises Lee and Jackson had in store for him. The commander has to have the confidence to follow a plan through, and the perception and flexibility to recognize when to change his plan. On April 30 and May 1, Hooker should have recognized that forcing Lee to attack him might have been a good idea, but not in the Wilderness, where the terrain negated the Federal advantage in numbers.

The most surprising thing about the Battle of Chancellorsville is that Jackson's flank attack on the second day did not win the battle for Lee. The Federals really started to lose the battle on the third day, when Sedgwick failed to move quickly, and Hooker failed to force him to move as quickly as he might have. Hooker made some tactical errors that same day, even before his injury, but the result was the Army of the Potomac being forced back into a very strong position that Lee would have had trouble attacking.

Edward G. Longacre, in his recent comparative study of Lee and Hooker at Chancellorsville,[42] compared them both to poker players. Longacre pointed out that at the start Lee took the approach of a chess player, carefully thinking out each of his moves in advance. In many ways, this is what Hooker also tried to do. His plans were not perfect, but they were good—if they were properly implemented. But on May 1, 1863, Hooker in effect tried to bluff Lee into attacking him, when he did not have to bluff. Lee then, Longacre says, seemed to join Hooker in poker, but he did it a lot better. Lee "called the bluff and his opponent promptly folded."[43] Hooker was behind, it has to be admitted, on May 5, when he conceded the match and retreated back across the Rappahannock-Rapidan line. But the game was not over.

Darius Couch agreed, as he wrote about twenty-five years later, in the collection of articles by various commanders called *Battles and Leaders of the Civil War*. "In looking for the causes of the loss of Chancellorsville, the primary ones were that Hooker expected Lee to fall back without risking battle. Finding himself mistaken he assumed the defensive, and was outgeneraled and became demoralized by the superior tactical boldness of the enemy."[44]

As to Hooker himself, there is a famous story as to Hooker's own explanation. The source is indirect, a 1903 letter (forty years after the fact) quoted in a 1910 history of the battle. The story is almost certainly not true, since Hooker and Doubleday probably did not cross paths, and it shows a degree of self-understanding Hooker lacked. The remark was supposedly overheard between General Hooker and General Abner Doubleday during the initial phases of the Gettysburg campaign, seven weeks after Chancellorsville. Doubleday asked Hooker what happened: Was he drunk or did a shell injure him? Hooker is supposed to have responded, "Doubleday, I was not hurt by a shell, and I was not drunk. For once I lost confidence in Hooker, and that is all there is to it."[45]

The story is probably false. But it also probably accurately explains what happened to Hooker.

6

GETTYSBURG

The Spin Shifts

The dogmas of the quiet past are inadequate to the stormy present.

—Abraham Lincoln, December 1, 1862[1]

The Battle of Chancellorsville ended on May 6, 1863, with Hooker and the Army of the Potomac slinking north across the Rappahannock/Rapidan line to safety. However, the Battle of the Wilderness did not immediately follow the Battle of Chancellorsville, with a pause only to change commanders. A year passed. And this was a very eventful year. Not only commanders had changed when the Army of the Potomac again moved into the Wilderness. The war was very much not over. The Western theater was usually a scene of Federal success. But we might say today, the spin in the East shifted.

Lee looked to follow up his victory at Chancellorsville. He began to seriously consider a second invasion of the North almost as soon as the Chancellorsville campaign had ended. Lee wanted to regain the strategic initiative, and to keep the momentum of victory going. Lee was concerned that the Federals might be able to find a general with the tactical skill, the determination, and the moral courage to be able to carry out what Hooker had intended in his turning movement.

Lee was not the only strategic thinker in Richmond at the time, and Virginia not the only front. Lee considered Virginia the main front. Things were going well in Virginia, but not elsewhere in the Confederacy. James Seddon, Confederate secretary of war, was among those starting to get worried about the West, particularly Vicksburg, Mississippi. Ulysses S. Grant was making another attempt at Vicksburg. On May 14, 1863, word reached Richmond that Grant's forces had taken Jackson, Mississippi, cutting Vicksburg's main link to the heart of the Confederacy. Federal forces approached Vicksburg, and it was uncertain the city could hold.

Seddon wanted to transfer some men from Lee's army to the West, to reinforce the forces trying to defend Vicksburg. Seddon had first raised this idea before the Battle of Chancellorsville. Lee had expressed reservations, pointing out technical problems in transferring forces so great a distance on the less than dependable Southern railroad system. He also said that weakening the Army of Northern Virginia might force him to leave the Fredericksburg area and retreat to Richmond. When the discussion picked up at a May 15, 1863, meeting between Lee, Seddon, and Confederate president Jefferson Davis, Lee said that a movement north by his army might help relieve pressure on Vicksburg by persuading the Lincoln administration to withdraw men and bring them East. As the Confederate spring campaign was planned and implemented, Grant seemed bogged down at Vicksburg. His initial attacks had failed, and he soon settled down to a siege. However, though he could not get into Vicksburg, thirty thousand or so Confederate soldiers could not get out.

As great as the victory at Chancellorsville seemed, Lee was not happy with the win. Casualties were heavy. His best subordinate commander, Stonewall Jackson, died not long after the battle. And Lee had not won the decisive battle he wanted to win. The Army of the Potomac, though badly damaged, was likely to try again.

Lee was always inclined to the offensive, and to seek to maintain the initiative. He felt that the South would lose a war of attrition, a war that let the North bring to bear its superior manpower and resources. Lee considered that battlefield victories would apply pressure to the North, particularly to public opinion, and convince the North that the South could not be defeated.

A pro-forma cabinet meeting was held to discuss Vicksburg on May 16; however, Davis had almost certainly given Lee permission to move north the day before. No record of the May 15 meeting exists.

Lee's problem of how to follow up and deal with success was preferable to the Northern problem of how to deal with yet another defeat in the East, particularly galling because the Chancellorsville campaign had started out with such hopes for success. President Lincoln's first reaction on hearing the news of the defeat at Chancellorsville was an anguished, "My God! What will the country say?"[2]

The Philadelphia Brigade, which had spent the battle on guard duty, returned to camp a day or two after fighting ended. Brigade staff, too tired to
weed through the week's backlog of announcements, read a now painfully
and perversely ironic announcement to the men, Hooker's general orders
of May 1: "The enemy must either ingloriously fly or come out from behind
his defenses and give us battle on our own ground."[3]

Unlike Lee, Hooker was losing the confidence of his superiors and his
subordinates. Abraham Lincoln visited the army on May 7, just the day
after the retreat across the Rapidan/Rappahannock line, to see the situation with the army for himself. He asked Hooker a simple question, "What
next? Have you already in your mind a plan wholly, or partially formed?"[4]
Hooker responded that he did have such a plan, but there is no indication
he gave details.

General in Chief Henry Halleck had accompanied Lincoln to visit
Hooker. Halleck stayed on a few days to meet with Hooker's corps and
division commanders. Halleck came back very gloomy about the army's
command situation under Hooker. But Lincoln faced the same problem he
had faced with McClellan—who could take over command from Hooker?
There were also political risks. McClellan had been popular with conservative elements. Hooker was popular with the more radical elements of the
Republican Party. Lincoln needed support from both.

Then the counts against Hooker began to pile up further. Lincoln reported some captured information to Hooker on May 8, almost immediately after Lincoln's return to Washington.

> General Willich, an exchanged prisoner, just from Richmond, has talked with
> me this morning. He was there when our cavalry cut the roads in that vicinity.
> He says there was not a sound pair of legs in Richmond, and that our men, had
> they known it, could have safely gone in and burned everything and brought
> in Jeff Davis.
>
> We captured and paroled 300 or 400 men. He says as he came to City Point
> there was an army 3 miles long (Longstreet's, he thought) moving toward
> Richmond. Milroy has captured a dispatch of General Lee, in which he says
> his loss was fearful in his last battle with you.[5]

Some sources say that Lincoln had more details on Lee's losses, and that
this may have provoked his comment to William Stoddard about more such
losses, which Stoddard remembered as just after the Battle of Fredericksburg.[6] Lincoln's statements are consistent with Lee's lack of enthusiasm
over his seemingly clear victory at Chancellorsville.

About a week later, when he learned that Hooker was considering a direct stab across the river at Fredericksburg, Lincoln discouraged the move, writing Hooker that the immediate time for such an attempt had passed. Lincoln was also displeased to hear that Hooker had started to inflate Lee's strength, McClellan style.

At the same May 13 meeting, Lincoln told Hooker that "I must tell you, that I have some painful intimations that your corps and division commanders are not giving you their entire confidence. This would be ruinous, if true."[7] This would also be a replay of the situation just before Hooker's predecessor, Ambrose Burnside, was relieved of command of the Army of the Potomac, which both Lincoln and Hooker would have realized. There were some major differences with the commanders, though. Many of the discontented senior commanders had left the army the same time Hooker took command. Hooker himself was a notable exception. George Meade, John Reynolds, and Darius Couch, though all unhappy with Hooker, would not have engaged in something like the plotting against Burnside.

There was a more important difference. The Army of the Potomac had been misused at Chancellorsville. However, it was still in better shape than when Hooker had taken command four months earlier. There was, as might be expected, some grumbling on the state of the army, but focusing on its poor leadership. One Federal wrote, "The Chancellorsville Campaign pretty thoroughly demonstrated the fact that as a general in the field at the head of an army, Gen. Joseph Hooker was no match for Gen. R. E. Lee."[8]

One Pennsylvania soldier wrote, in a letter published in a newspaper, "The talk about demoralization in this army is all false. The army is no more demoralized than the day it first started out, although God knows it has had, though the blundering of inefficient commanders and other causes too numerous to mention, plenty of reason to be."[9]

However, Lincoln, Secretary of War Stanton, and General Halleck decided that Hooker had to go. They began looking for a replacement. On May 22 Lincoln asked Darius Couch, senior general in the Army of the Potomac outside of Hooker, if he wanted the command. Couch, though agreeing that Hooker had to go, declined on grounds of health. He also asked to be relieved from service in the Army of the Potomac. Lincoln transferred Couch to command of the newly created Department of Pennsylvania. During the same meeting, Couch recommended putting George Meade in command.

John Reynolds met with Lincoln on June 1. He was asked his conditions for accepting command of the Army of the Potomac. Reynolds had one condition for accepting: that he would have no interference from the president or the War Department. Lincoln pointed out that this would not be possible. Reynolds later told Meade that he did not think Lincoln had then been looking to drop Hooker. Reynolds paraphrased Lincoln as saying, "He was not disposed to throw away a gun because it missed fire once; that he would pick the lock and try again."[10] The paraphrase sounds like Lincoln, though perhaps it was delivered to assure Reynolds that the question of command was only a "what if." One of Reynolds's aides was told that Reynolds had turned down the command on account of too much interference from Washington. However, by June 1 Lincoln was almost certainly looking for a reason to replace Hooker, not to let him fight another major battle.

On June 3, Lee's army began to move to the northwest, to the area of Culpeper, Virginia. The two of Longstreet's divisions at Fredericksburg moved first, followed a day later by Ewell's corps. Twenty thousand men of Hill's corps were left to watch the eighty thousand Federals. The Confederates moved at night, to try to hide their movements from the Federal balloon observers.

On June 4, however, the Federals realized that something was up. "The rascals are up to something," a I Corps staff officer wrote in his diary that day.[11] The next day Lee, still in the area, told Hill to do what he could to deceive the Federals as to the army's movement. If forced to retreat from Fredericksburg, Hill would fall back to the North Anna River and link up with Pickett's division.

Late that afternoon, a small body of Federal troops crossed the Rappahannock River, while a verbal exchange was underway between Hooker on one side, Lincoln and Halleck on the other. Hooker thought that if Lee was headed north with most of his army, this was the time to attack across the river, and even stab toward Richmond. Hooker was willing to risk having Lee's army threaten Washington. Lincoln was not. By the end of June 5, however, Hooker had crossed a force of about a division, from Sedgwick's VI Corps, a probing effort to try to find out Lee's strength in the area.

However, on June 6 the Federal force just sat. Sedgwick was authorized to throw his entire corps across the river, but he decided to limit the force to the initial one division. Hooker was somewhat indecisive about what this force was to do, observe or serve as the lead element of an attack to the south. But if he wanted Sedgwick to do more, he would have been advised to order, rather than just suggest, sending over more men.

Some skirmishing occurred on June 10, but there was little activity otherwise. Lincoln had reminded Hooker that Lee's army was his main objective, not Richmond. Hooker took this as lack of approval for aiming at

Richmond. Sedgwick's men and Hill's men both soon joined the movement north of the rest of their armies.

Robert E. Lee brought several problems with him when he headed north, which he seems not to have properly evaluated.

First: Perhaps most importantly, Lee was invading the North with a greatly reorganized army. Lee had been considering some changes even before Chancellorsville, but the reorganization after that battle was prompted by the need to replace Stonewall Jackson, mortally wounded at the Battle of Chancellorsville. Lee had reorganized his army into three corps, from the previous two. Richard Ewell and A. P. Hill were the new corps commanders. Other command changes occurred at division and brigade level, with at least half these commands held by new commanders.

Lee should have allowed himself time to get used to the new system, particularly to Ewell and Hill. They had served well in the past, though Ewell was just going back onto active duty after recovering from a major wound. They were not as good as Jackson, but few generals were. More importantly, Ewell and Hill were different than Jackson, and had to be managed differently by Lee. However, Lee was aware that if he waited, Northern forces would move into Virginia for the spring/summer campaign. An invasion of the North would temporarily remove pressure from Virginia.

Second: When the Gettysburg campaign got underway, Lee was traveling blind, though he need not have been. Confederate cavalry should have been screening the main army. However, Lee's orders to his usually effective cavalry commander, Stuart, were too discretionary. Stuart went far to the east of the Federal Army of the Potomac, and got cut off by the unexpected northward movement of this army. One of Lee's aides later wrote, "An army without cavalry in a strange and hostile country is as a man deprived of his eyesight and beset by enemies; he may be never so brave and strong, but he cannot intelligently administer a single effective blow."[12]

Interestingly, Lee had considered keeping Stuart in command of Jackson's old corps. Stuart had done a good job the last three days at Chancellorsville. Lee decided that Stuart was too valuable in control of the cavalry. A historical "what if," a possible tipping point, is what might have happened at Gettysburg if Stuart had been in command of either Ewell's corps or Hill's corps, and Wade Hampton, Stuart's second in command, had been running the cavalry.

Even with Stuart missing, Lee, however, still had about half his cavalry, enough to remedy his operational problems. But Lee lacked the cavalry commander he most trusted and on whom he most depended.

Third: Lee failed to immediately recognize the implications of the June 28, 1863, change in Federal commanders, from Joseph Hooker to the less flashy, perhaps less creative, but steadier George Meade. Lincoln, Secretary of War Edwin Stanton, and General in Chief Henry Halleck had been determined that Hooker not command the Army of the Potomac in another major battle. Hooker would later be cited for skillfully maneuvering his army and covering Washington during the first phases of the campaign. However, when Hooker submitted his resignation over the issue of being denied control over the Federal garrison at Harpers Ferry, it was immediately accepted.

Meade would better respond to changing situations than Hooker. Lee likely could not have changed strategic or operational plans in two days, but he might have adopted more defensive and less offensive tactics. Lee's nature, however, particularly when it could logically be argued that in enemy territory the Confederates had to maintain the initiative, pushed him toward the offensive. Meade had the advantage of not having to make changes in his army, aside from his own replacement as commander of the V Corps by George Sykes.

Finally: Lee came to Gettysburg with unrealistic confidence in his men and what they could accomplish. Confederate soldiers in the Army of Northern Virginia, whatever one thinks of the morality of their cause, were among the best soldiers ever. But they were not perfect. They could not win everywhere, they could not capture every ridge, could not do what could not be done. Their commander had the responsibility of knowing what not to ask.

The Battle of Gettysburg was a "meeting engagement"—both armies were on the move; both commanders had to respond to the sudden opportunity to give battle. The Confederate Army of Northern Virginia, under Robert E. Lee, was engaged in a massive thrust into Federal territory. The Federal Army of the Potomac, under Joseph Hooker and then under George Meade, was in pursuit, seeking to catch and give battle to Lee's army while always staying between that army and Washington, D.C. Neither expected to make contact that Wednesday, July 1, 1863, in the small Pennsylvania town of Gettysburg, though both knew a battle was imminent.

Fighting at Gettysburg began early on Wednesday, July 1, 1863. The actual tactical decision to send Southern troops into Gettysburg, taken the night before, seems to have had an oddly casual air to it. A Confederate scout had reported the presence of Federal cavalry in Gettysburg, speculating that the detachment was trained troops, not militia. The senior Confederate general on the scene, Hill, did not accept this report. Major General Henry Hatch, one of Hill's division commanders, told Hill, "If there is no objection. I will take my division to-morrow and go to Gettysburg." Hill, who wanted to deny Gettysburg as a base to the Federals, and also wanted to be sure what was in his front, responded, "None in the world."[13]

After fighting started the next morning, Hill and Heth fed in troops despite not knowing what they faced, and despite having been instructed not to bring on a general engagement with the Federals. Lee, who arrived at Gettysburg about midday July 1, then thought he had no choice but to send in more troops. In the words of Lee's official report on the Battle of Gettysburg,

> It had not been intended to deliver a general battle so far from our base unless attacked, but coming unexpectedly upon the whole Federal army, to withdraw through the mountains with our extensive trains would have been difficult and dangerous. At the same time we were unable to await attack, as the county was unfavorable for collecting supplies in the presence of the enemy. . . . A battle, had, therefore become in a measure unavoidable, and the success already gained gave hope of a favorable issue.[14]

War has its own momentum. The job of the commander is to determine whether to go with the momentum, or resist. Looking only at the facts available at the time, Lee's decision to fight the battle at Gettysburg is understandable, but still debatable.

Despite five changes in their senior commander on the scene, the Federals held their own most of the first day. They were eventually outflanked by the Confederates and driven south through Gettysburg itself. That afternoon and evening two major command decisions were made, one possibly and one likely affecting the eventual outcome of the Battle of Gettysburg.

Later that day Lee told Richard Ewell, Second Corps commander, to capture Culp's Hill, just south of the town, "if practicable." Ewell considered the attack not practicable. Perhaps he was right, as the Federals had already started to entrench. Lee's discretionary order was in keeping with his command practices. Lee himself once described his job as getting the army to the battlefield, and then letting his chief subordinates fight the battle. He, and others, had no justification for later complaining about Ewell's actions, or inaction. Whether Ewell's judgment was correct, Ewell had followed orders.

On the Federal side, a command decision made earlier by George Meade paid off late that afternoon. Meade had sent Major General Winfield Scott Hancock, commander of the II Corps, to take over at Gettysburg until Meade himself could reach the battlefield. Hancock was junior to XI Corps commander Oliver Howard, the fourth Federal commander at Gettysburg that day. In selecting Hancock, Meade used his newly granted authority to appoint subordinates to command positions regardless of seniority. Hancock recognized the combination of Cemetery Ridge, Cemetery Hill, and Culp's Hill as a strong position, a position where the retreating Federals could rally and one that they could hold.

Lee not only had problems with discretionary orders at Gettysburg. He also had problems getting specific orders carried out. Starting the first night, Lee had to deal with a recalcitrant subordinate, James Longstreet, who did not want to attack. "If the enemy is there tomorrow, we must attack him,"[15] Lee told Longstreet, according to Longstreet, writing after the war. Longstreet, again by his own account, replied, "If he is there, it will be because he is anxious we should attack him—a good reason in my judgment for not doing so."[16]

The Confederates had problems getting attacks started the next day. The main area of Confederate efforts, attacks on the Federal left, did not start until 4 p.m. on July 2, only four hours before sunset. The attacks still might have worked, because one Federal corps, the III, was out of position. Daniel Sickles, "Sickles the Incredible" as he was called, did not like the position to which his command had been assigned. He moved his men forward, without telling Meade. Fortunately for the Federal cause, Sickles was wounded in the battle. Hancock took over Sickles's Third Corps as well as his own Second Corps. Hancock's expert tactics blunted strong Confederate efforts, and saved that section of the Federal line, and possibly the battle. Effective improvisation means knowing when as well as how to improvise.

At about the same time, another potentially fatal Federal error was corrected at Little Round Top, a small hill dominating the Federal left. Meade sent his chief engineer, Brigadier General Gouverneur Kemble Warren, to check this area. Warren found only a few guns, and some men, on the hill. They were getting ready to withdraw the guns. Warren had one artillery piece fire a shell into some woods not far from the hill. In Warren's words,

> As the shot went whistling through the air the sound of it reached the enemy's troops and caused every one to look in the direction of it. This motion revealed to me the glistening of gun-barrels and bayonets of the enemy's line of battle, already formed and far outflanking the position of any of our troops; so that the line of his advance from his right to Little Round Top was unopposed.[17]

Warren immediately sent an aide to Sickles, asking that a division be sent to occupy Little Round Top. Sickles refused, saying that he could not spare any men. (Sickles's change of position had put his corps in such trouble that he likely could not spare any men.) Warren had anticipated this, and had already sent a messenger directly to Meade. Sykes and the V Corps were on their way to reinforce Sickles. Meade changed Sykes's orders and told him to bring his corps to the left of the Federal lines.

Warren grew impatient and went to look for Sykes. He found that Sykes had ridden ahead of his men to see for himself the III Corps position and where his corps would be needed—as originally ordered by Meade. After speaking with Warren, Sykes now sent an order to General Barnes, commanding the V Corps' First Division, to send a brigade to Little Round Top. Colonel Strong Vincent, one of Barnes's brigade commanders, soon spotted Sykes's aide searching for Barnes.

Oliver W. Norton, a witness to the conversation, later wrote:

> Vincent, who evidently knew the captain, left the head of his brigade and rode forward to meet him. . . . Arriving, Vincent said, "Captain, what are your orders?" Without replying directly, the officer said, "Where is General Barnes?" If Vincent knew he did not answer the question, but said with emphasis: "What are your orders? Give me your orders." The officer replied, "General Sykes directed me to tell General Barnes to occupy that hill yonder," [pointing] to Little Round Top. Without a moment's hesitation, Vincent replied, "I will take the responsibility of taking my brigade there."[18]

Led by Colonel Joshua Chamberlain's 20th Maine, Vincent's brigade reached the hill from the northwest, climbing the northern slope, within view of Confederate artillery. As Chamberlain later wrote,

> The enemy's artillery got range of our column as we were climbing the spur, and the crashing of the shells among the rocks and treetops made us move lively along the crest.
>   Passing to the southern slope of Little Round Top, Colonel Vincent indicated to me the ground my regiment was to occupy, informing me that this was the extreme left of our general line, and that a desperate attack was expected in order to turn the position, concluding by telling me that I was to "hold the ground at all hazards." . . . That was the last word I heard from him. . . . In order to commence by making my right firm, I formed my regiment on the right into line, giving such directions to the line as would best secure the advantage.[19]

Company B of the 20th Maine, commanded by Captain Walter G. Morrill, was dispatched to serve as a skirmish line on the 20th Maine's left flank.

Chamberlain and his men almost immediately became involved in fighting, as parts of Robertson's and Law's brigades attacked the center of

Vincent's line. Chamberlain's narration continues: "The artillery fire on our position had meanwhile been constant and heavy, but my formation was scarcely complete when the artillery was replaced by a vigorous assault upon the center of our brigade to my right, but it very soon involved the right of my regiment and gradually extended along my entire front. The action was quite sharp and at close quarters."[20]

About this time William Oates and his 15th Alabama came off Big Round Top. Oates and his men had been working their way around the entire left of the Federal line. The Confederates had come under direct fire after crossing Plumb Run at the base of Big Round Top—a higher hill, but far more tree covered and thus less dominant than Little Round Top. Oates narrates his regiment's adventures at this point:

> Our whole line advanced in quick time, under the fire of our guns, through the valley which lay before us at the foot of the range of [Big Round Top and Little Round Top], with a small muddy meandering stream running through it. . . . When crossing the little run we received the first fire from the Federal infantry. . . . Our line did not halt, but pressing forward drove our enemy from the fence and up the side of the mountain. [After the two regiments to his right were moved to the left] This left my regiment on the extreme right flank of Lee's army, and as I advanced up the mountain side my right was soon exposed to a flank fire from Federal skirmishers which I promptly met by deploying my right company at short distances. I continued to advance up the southern face of Round Top. My men had to climb up, catching to the bushes and crawling over the immense boulders, in the fact of an incessant fire of their enemy who kept falling back, taking shelter and firing down on us from behind rocks and crags that covered the mountain side thicker than grave stones in a city cemetery.
>
> In this manner I pressed forward until I reached the top and the highest point on top of Round Top. Just before reaching this point, the Federals in my front as suddenly disappeared from my sight as though commanded by a magician.[21]

Just before his regiment started to advance, after very little rest, Oates dispatched two men from each company in his regiment, a total of twenty-two men, to take the regimental canteens and get water. The men were not able to return before the regiment advanced. Oates later learned that the canteen bearers had tried to follow the regiment, gotten lost, and accidentally wandered into Union lines. In his 1905 book, Oates credits lack of water as a major factor in the failure to take Little Round Top.[22]

The Federal sharpshooters were chased up and off Big Round Top. Oates and his men quickly advanced down Big Round Top to a small, relatively open area between the two hills. The view had not been particularly good from the top of the tree-covered Big Round Top. However, about two hundred or three hundred yards to the northeast of his position between the two hills, Oates noticed some unprotected Federal supply trains. Oates thought his men were hitting behind Federal lines as they approached Little Round Top. "After I had reached the level ground . . . in plain view of the Federal wagon trains, and within two hundred yards of an extensive park of Federal ordnance wagons, which satisfied me that I was then in the Federal rear, rapidly advancing, without any skirmishers in front. I saw no enemy, until within forty or fifty steps of an irregular ledge of rocks."[23] It was then that the 20th Maine opened fire.

When Colonel Chamberlain was told of the Confederates' approach, he climbed onto a large rock and saw the severe danger to his, and the army's, left flank. His regiment was taking fire from the attack on Vincent's right and was unable to fully change front. Chamberlain proceeded to have each man move to the left a few feet, and then "refused" the left—bending half of the regiment backward until it formed almost a right angle with the rest of the regiment. Taking good advantage of the rough ground, the 20th Maine now occupied a front twice the size it had originally taken up just a few moments before.

To again quote Chamberlain:

> My officers and men understood my wishes so well that its movement was executed under fire, the right wing keeping up fire, without giving the enemy any occasion to seize or even to suspect their advantage. But we were not a moment too soon; the enemy's flanking column, having gained their desired direction, burst upon my left, where they evidently had expected an unguarded flank, with great determination.[24]

While still helping with the fighting on Vincent's right, the 20th Maine opened a heavy fire on the attacking Confederates. Oates's men fell back to the shelter of rocks and low trees in the valley between the two Round Tops. The Confederates soon charged again, coming to within a dozen yards of the Federals, but they were again driven back.

The Alabamians soon attacked again, and the fighting became severe. The fighting was hand to hand at places where Chamberlain's line was temporarily breached. Men on both sides used their rifles as clubs. Brief pauses in the fighting were used to gather ammunition from the dead and wounded of both sides.

Commanded by an officer equally as determined as Chamberlain, the Confederates began a fifth assault on the 20th Maine's lines. This attack was slowed by Chamberlain's men firing their remaining ammunition,[25] and by the 47th Alabama, covering Oates's left though focusing on the regiment to Chamberlain's right, giving way. However, the 20th Maine probably could not resist a sixth attack. Chamberlain later wrote the governor of Maine about what happened next:

> Our loss had been so great, and the remain[ing] men were so much exhausted, having fire[d] all our "sixty rounds" and all the cartridges we could gather from the scattered bones of the fallen around us, friend and foe, I saw no way left but to take the offensive.[26]

According to Chamberlain's official report:

> At that crisis I ordered the bayonet. The word was enough. It ran like fire along the line and rose into a shout, with which they spring forward upon the enemy, now not 30 yards away. The effect was surprising; many of the enemy's first line threw down their arms and surrendered. An officer fired his pistol at my head with one hand, while he handed me his sword with the other. Holding fast by our right and swinging forward our left, we made an extended right wheel, before which the enemy's second line broke and fell back, fighting from tree to tree, many being captured, until we had swept the valley and cleared the front of nearly our entire brigade.[27]

There was later some controversy over whether Chamberlain actually gave the order to charge, or whether his men acted on their own. This does not really matter. The action was a desperate move to stave off defeat, but it was also an effective way to adapt to an emergency situation. Whatever the motives, whoever gave the order, or whether the men took the action without orders, it worked.

Morrill's Company B, and the sharpshooters earlier chased off Big Round Top, now reappeared in the story. They rose from behind a stone wall where they had been pinned and fired into the Confederate left flank. Oates wrote, "With a withering and deadly fire poured in upon us from every direction, it seemed that the entire command was doomed to destruction. . . . I did order a retreat, but did not undertake to retire in order. I had the officers and men advised that when the signal was given every one should run in the direction from whence he came, and halt on top of the mountain."[28] Oates reported having gone into action with 700 men, having 225 left when the fight ended. Chamberlain and his 20th Maine lost 130 men of the 330 it took into battle.

The second day's fighting did not end when Chamberlain stopped his men from charging too far away from Federal lines, nor when G. K. Warren again "saved the day" by plugging a hole that developed on the west slope of Little Round Top. "Peach orchard" and "wheatfield" would take on new meanings, reflective of the fierce and bloody fighting in which Federal forces barely held.

The last Confederate force to attack that day, Ambrose Wright's brigade, almost made it to the "copse of trees," the aiming point the next day for Pickett's Charge, before being bloodily ejected by Federal reinforcements. Wright was asked about this the next day. He responded, "The trouble is not in going there. I went there with my brigade yesterday. . . . The trouble is to stay there after you get there, for the whole Yankee army is there in a bunch."[29]

On the second day of the battle, Lee, whose forces were attacking, should have improvised more than he did and ensured the same from his immediate subordinates, but he did not. Meade and his subordinates, with the notable exception of Daniel Sickles, picked the right times to adapt and to improvise. As a result, the battle was still raging the next day for one of the most famous incidents in military history, Pickett's Charge. Whether that charge should have been ordered, whether by the third day Lee had any alternatives, is still debated, a debate greatly influenced by the fact that it failed.

George Pickett's division of Virginia troops were not the only Confederate soldiers who took part in the final Confederate attack at Gettysburg, the afternoon of the third day of the battle. But Pickett has given his name to Pickett's Charge.

Lee's plan for the charge was not a bad one. After a lengthy artillery preparation, roughly two hours as it turned out, a large force of Confederate troops would smash their way through a weakened portion of the Federal lines—in this case the center. Further Confederate troops were designated for possible flank support of the attacking column. If delivered with sufficient force and sufficient speed, Lee's plan had elements in common with the World War II tactic that came to be called blitzkrieg. However, this tactic depended on breaking through with enough men to create a significant opening, on further troops arriving to exploit the opening and prevent its repair by the defenders, and on cavalry arriving to spread panic and confusion in the defenders' rear. Primarily this tactic depends on defenders being too demoralized to repair the breach in their defenses, cut off the penetrating force, and use reserve units to demolish that force.

Lee's plan began to go wrong almost at the start. The lengthy opening artillery bombardment overshot the Federal front lines, leaving troops, and artillery, pretty much intact. Federal commanders were uncertain whether to return fire. Henry Hunt, artillery commander, wanted to save ammunition to use against the inevitable infantry charge. Winfield Scott Hancock, commanding the II Corps, the target of the Confederate attack, wanted Federal artillery to fire to keep up the morale of his troops.

This dispute may have led to the best of both worlds for the Federals. Since Hancock ranked Hunt, the guns fired. But many began to run low on ammunition. Hunt had them stop firing. He also rotated some of the batteries. When the Confederates saw this, to the degree the black powder of the day did not obscure any view, they thought the barrage had accomplished its goal. The infantry was ordered to advance.

The attacking forces left the tree line almost a mile from the Federal position. They immediately came under fire from more distant Federal positions on Little Round Top and Culp's Hill. About halfway through the charge they began to take heavy, and effective, fire from the still quite strong Federal positions on Cemetery Ridge.

Lee's intent was for the attack to be focused on a Federal front a few hundred yards wide. The mile-wide attack lines had to narrow their advance as they approached Federal lines. Despite appearances, Confederate and Federal lines were not parallel, so different units had to advance at different speeds. They were also attacking uphill. There were problems coordinating the many units involved, and the varying directions of advance.

Fences on the Emmitsburg Road also delayed the advance, as they had to be taken down. Surprisingly, at this point it appears that many of the attacking soldiers just gave up and went back to the Confederate lines. Others remained, to be caught in a "cauldron" formed when Federal troops could flank them on both sides. Several Confederate brigades designated for flank support did advance part of the way. They were called back when James Longstreet saw the attack was failing and that he would just be causing unnecessary casualties. The morale of some of the men in the first wave was not helped when they saw the support units turn back. A third Confederate effort that day, a simultaneous attempt to move cavalry into Meade's rear, was stopped several miles east of the main battlefield.

Was Pickett's Charge a reasonable risk?

A recent historian has written that, a bit melodramatically,

Properly led on the decisive afternoon at Gettysburg, George Pickett's Virginians and Johnston Pettigrew's Carolinians would not have been sent against across the killing fields from Seminary to Cemetery Ridge, against the massed Union army. But their bravery at Chancellorsville had persuaded their general that they were invincible, and so he had sent them. And so Gettysburg was lost, and so the war.[30]

James Longstreet, for all the controversy about his actions at Gettysburg, probably got it correct when he later wrote, "One mistake of the Confederacy was in pitting force against force. The only hope we had was to outgeneral the Federals."[31]

Another recent historian writes, "If July 1 was the battle of accidental encounters and July 2 the fight for dominant position, then the combat on July 3 was driven solely by Robert E. Lee's desire for a decisive victory."[32] Once Lee saw that he would not be able to effectively strike the Federal left, and with the town of Gettysburg and Culp's Hill making a full effort against the Federal right unrealistic, an attack on the Federal center became almost inevitable, given Lee's aggressive nature and the reasonable possibility Meade would attack if Lee did not. Lee did not want to just sit. However, on July 4, 1863, that is exactly what Lee did, with no Federal attack, but on the morning of July 3 the Federals had not yet suffered the losses of Pickett's Charge.

George Meade has taken criticism, starting almost when the third day of fighting ended, for not following up the repulse of Pickett's Charge. Just as Lee's nature made the attack almost inevitable, the lack of immediate follow-up was almost inevitable from a cautious Federal commander. Even had he thought of attacking, Meade saw that his army had also been heavily damaged. His most aggressive corps commander, Hancock, had been wounded in Pickett's Charge. Lee also still held a very strong position, and would have had a good chance at beating back any counterattack. Meade cannot be faulted for deciding to settle for the notable victory he had won.

Lee's army withdrew from Gettysburg on a very rainy July 4, 1863, the same day Vicksburg surrendered to Grant. About a week later, Lee's army was backed up against the Potomac, too swollen from heavy rains to cross. Lee, however, was in a very strong position, and Meade delayed attacking until he could fully study the position.

Lincoln's son Robert, about twenty years later, said that Lincoln drafted a preemptory order for Meade to attack at the Potomac. Robert Lincoln said that Meade was told if the attack was successful he should destroy the order, but if it failed he could keep it as evidence that he had been acting on the instructions of the president.[33] No other evidence has been found on Lincoln's action, or a copy of this order.

Crushing Pickett's Charge may not have been the military turning point of the Civil War in the East most people think. However, when the Federals smashed the charge, they destroyed the myth of invincibility incalculably valuable to Lee and the Army of Northern Virginia. Lee had shown he was human, capable of management and command errors, capable of being slow to accept and slow to adapt to change. Lee had learned the wrong lessons from Chancellorsville. He believed his army was invincible. The Army of Northern Virginia was one of the best armies ever. But it was not invincible. The "spin" had started to shift. Yankee commanders, and perhaps more importantly Yankee soldiers, now thought they could win. This was a key tipping point in the war. The war, however, had not ended.

The next few months after Gettysburg, and Meade's slow pursuit of Lee, through the end of November, were occupied by indecisive maneuvering of both armies. A major attack almost occurred at Mine Run, on November 30, 1863, when at the last minute Meade canceled a frontal assault on strong Confederate positions. Canceling this attack appears to have revived Meade's flagging popularity with the Army of the Potomac. When Grant arrived and took over effective control—though Meade remained in command until the end of the war—Grant received an army in much better shape than Hooker had received from Burnside.

A strange follow-up to Pickett's Charge occurred in 1870. John Mosby, the famous Confederate partisan leader, went with George Pickett for a brief meeting with Robert E. Lee. The meeting did not go well. A few moments after leaving, Pickett muttered something about the old man who had his division massacred at Gettysburg. Mosby responded, somewhat angrily, "Well, it made you immortal," and walked away.[34]

7

THE LAST COMMAND TRANSITION?

I write this now as a grateful acknowledgement for the almost inestimable service you have done the country.

—Abraham Lincoln, 1863[1]

A solution to his problem of finding the type of commander he needed began to present itself to Lincoln the very day Lee left Gettysburg, July 4, 1863, retreating to Virginia. Lincoln may have first started thinking about the solution when he drafted messages to the successful Federal commanders at Gettysburg and at Vicksburg.

Vicksburg, Mississippi, the most important Southern position on the Mississippi River, surrendered to Federal forces under Ulysses S. Grant on July 4, 1863. The situation for the North in the West in the Civil War, basically Tennessee, Mississippi, Georgia, and Kentucky, was almost the opposite of that in Virginia. Northern commanders were usually better than their counterparts in Virginia. Fighting against Confederates usually inferior in talents to Lee and his subordinates, the Federal generals won most of their battles.

Grant became the most prominent Federal commander in the West, though that theater also produced William Sherman, George Thomas, and Philip Sheridan, all of whom became famous the last year of the war. Grant was caught by a surprise attack at Shiloh, Tennessee, April 1862, but Federal reinforcements, the death of the Southern commander, and Grant's own determination enabled him to totally reverse the course of the battle.

The evening of the first day at Shiloh, one of Grant's aides came to him to report on the state of the army after a day of savage fighting. When the aide then asked Grant if he was going to order a retreat, the normally placid Grant strongly responded, "No! I propose to attack at daylight and whip them."[2] Grant's career indicates that this calm confidence was the real Grant. This is the mark of a first-rate general. But if Grant here, and in a similar remark to Sherman, was putting on a show of confidence, this is also the mark of a first-rate commander.

William Sherman once analyzed Grant to another officer. Sherman said that "I'm a damned sight smarter man than Grant; I know a great deal more about war, military history, strategy, and grand tactics than he does; I know more about organization, supply and administration and about everything else than he does; but I'll tell you where he beats me and where he beats the world. He don't care a damn for what the enemy does out of his sight, but it scares me like hell."[3]

Sherman added,

> I am more nervous than he is. I am more likely to change my orders or to countermarch my command than he is. He uses such information as he has according to his best judgment; he issues his orders and does his level best to carry them out without much reference to what is going on about him and, so far, experience seems to have fully justified him.[4]

In his memoirs, Grant wrote that Shiloh changed his overall view on how to win the war. "Up to the battle of Shiloh I, as well as thousands of other citizens, believed that the rebellion against the Government would collapse suddenly and soon, if a decisive victory could be gained over any of its armies. . . . [After the battle, and Confederate counteroffensive of which it was a part] I gave up all idea of saving the Union except by complete conquest."[5]

The Battle of Shiloh took place just a few weeks before Ulysses S. Grant's fortieth birthday. Entering the United States Military Academy at West Point in 1839, he graduated twenty-first in a class of thirty-nine. At best an average student, Grant was particularly good in mathematics and art, and was an exceptionally good horseman. Grant opposed the Mexican War, which broke out in 1846, as did Abraham Lincoln. Grant decided not to resign from the army, however, and served with distinction in the war.

Marrying Julia Dent in 1848, Grant entered a peacetime army career. In 1854, after two years of service on the West Coast without his family, Grant resigned. Reports, even at the time, were that Grant left to avoid problems within the military from his heavy drinking. There is, however, little direct evidence.

Grant had a very undistinguished civilian career. When the American Civil War broke out, Grant was working in his father's leather and hardware store in Galena, Illinois. Trying to regain a commission, Grant received little immediate positive reaction. Finally, on June 17, 1861, with the assistance of Congressman Elihu B. Washburne, who represented the district in which Galena was located, Grant received a colonel's commission and a regimental command.

Grant's Civil War military career started with winning the Battle of Belmont, Missouri, on November 7, 1861. Three months later he gained national fame in capturing Fort Henry and Fort Donelson. The latter battle included Grant's statement that the only terms he would give the Confederates were "unconditional and immediate surrender," which brought Grant his first national attention. Grant was briefly "on the shelf" after Shiloh, when Henry Halleck took over active command of the armies under Grant and Don Carlos Buell. Grant was made second in command of the unified army, with little actual responsibilities. In June Halleck was called to Washington to become general in chief, and Grant regained active command of the main western armies.

Grant soon began his long, and slow, attempt to capture Vicksburg. At one point, he and General Sherman even tried to change topography to capture the city. Vicksburg sat on a bend of the Mississippi, where the river flowed east for a few miles, then turned around and flowed west back almost to where it had headed east. The river then resumed its southern course. In early spring of 1863 Grant and Sherman decided to dig a canal between the two bends of the river. They might not capture Vicksburg, but they would destroy its value to the Confederacy. The canal digging served only to keep their men occupied until active campaigning could resume. However, about twenty years later, the digging did work. The Mississippi, whose course changes from time to time, broke through and began flowing through the canal. Vicksburg now sits several miles away from the Mississippi River, which it had so dominated.

Grant finally decided on a long swing around the town, and an approach from the east. In late April, he moved his troops south of Vicksburg, on the west side of the Mississippi River. On April 29, Admiral David Porter's ships ran past Vicksburg. The next day they began to ferry Grant's army across the river. A Federal sergeant described the scene:

The sun rose throwing an impressive splendor upon the exciting scenes of the early morn. Every boat—transport and barge—lies at the landing, about five miles above Grand Gulf, covered till they are black with troops. Every heart here is full of anxiety and emotion; wondering eyes and eyes not altogether tearless, gaze ever and anon upon the *Father of Waters* [italics in original] where lies the formidable fleet of gunboats and rams, transports and barges, the latter heavily loaded with troops whose courage and valor are sufficient, when combined with that of the rest of this mighty army to redeem this lovely valley of the Mississippi.[6]

In the next seventeen days, as Grant's army swung to the north and then the east, the Federals won eleven battles or engagements. By May 18, 1863, Federals had cut off Vicksburg. After several days of heavy fighting and unsuccessful attacks, Grant settled down for a siege.

The siege grew tighter and tighter over the next weeks. Soldiers ran out of rations and ate horses and mules. The dog and rat population of the town began to decrease. Civilians lived in caves. One wrote in her diary:

Terror stricken, we remained crouched in the cave, while shell after shell followed each other in quick succession. I endeavored by constant prayer to prepare myself for the sudden death I was almost certain awaited me. My heart stood still as we would hear the reports from the guns, and the rushing and fearful sound of the shell as it came toward us.

As it neared, the noise became more deafening; the air was full of the rushing sound; pains darted through my temples; my ears were full of the confusing noise; and, as it exploded, the report flashed through my head like an electric shock, leaving me in a quiet state of terror the most painful I can imagine—cowering in a corner, holding my child to my breast—the only feeling of my life being the choking limbs of my heart, that rendered me almost breathless.[7]

On July 13, 1863, about a week after the July 4 fall of Vicksburg, Lincoln wrote Grant: "I write this now as a grateful acknowledgement for the almost inestimable service you have done the country."[8] Lincoln went on to say that he had questioned whether Grant should have joined Nathaniel Banks with a Federal army in Louisiana instead of going at Vicksburg. "I now wish to make the personal acknowledgement that you were right and I was wrong."[9] The only words of criticism Lincoln felt it necessary to send were aimed at Lincoln himself.

Lincoln ended up with a somewhat different message to the commander of Federal forces at Gettysburg, also a Federal victory. On July 14, 1863, the day after he sent the unequivocal congratulatory message to Grant,

Lincoln heard from George Meade about the progress in going after Lee's army. Lincoln received word that Lee and his army had been able to escape across the Potomac River, after a few days of sitting, though in strongly entrenched positions, between the rain-swollen river and the Army of the Potomac, without further damage. Lincoln is quoted as responding, "We had them in our grasp. We had only to stretch forth our hands and they were ours. And nothing I could say or do could make the Army move."[10] The next day he drafted a letter to George Meade, the winner at Gettysburg.

> I have just seen your dispatch to General Halleck, asking to be relieved of your command because of a supposed censure of mine. I am very, very grateful to you for the magnificent success you gave the cause of the country at Gettysburg; and I am sorry now to be the author of the slightest pain to you. But I was in such deep distress myself that I could not restrain some expression of it. I have been oppressed nearly ever since the battles at Gettysburg by what appeared to be evidences that yourself [and two cooperating, primarily local militia, Federal forces] were not seeking a collision with the enemy, but were trying to get him across the river without another battle. . . . I do not believe you appreciate the magnitude of the misfortune involved in Lee's escape. He was within your easy grasp, and to have closed upon him would, in connection with our other late successes, have ended the war. As it is, the war will be prolonged indefinitely. . . I beg you will not consider this a prosecution or persecution of yourself. As you had learned I was dissatisfied, I have thought it best to kindly tell you why.[11]

On reflection, Lincoln realized that at Gettysburg Meade had won the first clear victory over Robert E. Lee of any Federal commander. He also realized that Meade's army had been seriously weakened, and Lee's army was still dangerous. Meade should not be sent such a letter, which might have provoked his resignation. The letter was put in Lincoln's files, marked "To General Meade, never sent or signed." However, Lee and his army remained in the field. Despite his valuable services to the nation, Lincoln was beginning to see that Meade was not the answer to his problem.

On September 19 and 20, 1863, the Confederate Army of Tennessee defeated the Union Army of the Cumberland in fierce fighting at Chickamauga Creek, in northern Georgia. The Union army retreated northward, to Chattanooga, Tennessee. The Southern army began to besiege the place, though the supply lines were never cut off. In mid-November, about two months after the siege began, a substantially reinforced Federal army, under Grant's direct command, relieved the siege and dealt a major defeat to the Confederate forces.

This victory prompted Illinois congressman Elihu B. Washburne, a friend of Lincoln and the man who had gotten Grant his first Civil War commission, to introduce a bill reviving the rank of lieutenant general, last held by George Washington. After passage by Congress, and Lincoln's signature, Grant was formally promoted to this rank as of March 2, 1864. He was appointed general in chief of the Union army ten days later.

President Abraham Lincoln knew he needed a tough commander, able to coordinate all the Federal armies, East and West. He needed a persistent commander who would grab hold of Lee's army, take the punishment the Southerners could offer, the casualties they would inflict, and not let go until the war ended in a Union victory. He hoped Grant was the man he needed.

Grant seemed a less dynamic and popular man than Robert E. Lee. Grant frequently did not make a good first impression on people. After their first meeting, George Meade wrote his wife that Grant was "not a striking man, is very reticent, has never mixed with the world, indeed is somewhat ill at ease in the presence of strangers; hence a first impression is never favorable."[12] Meade offered to resign as commander of the Army of the Potomac, to allow Grant to put a western general in his place. Grant was impressed with Meade's devotion to duty and decided Meade would remain in command. Both Meade and Grant ended their first meeting with good impressions of each other.

Some in the Army of the Potomac, and outside of the army, were worried about Grant's reputation for having a drinking problem. But this was not really held against a general in the Army of the Potomac. As Bruce Catton has pointed out, "A general who never got drunk was a rarity—so much so that his sobriety was always mentioned in his biography, as a sign that he stood above the common run."[13] In addition, there is little actual evidence that Grant had a drinking problem at this time. Lincoln is supposed to have been told about Grant's drinking when Grant was still west. Lincoln responded, according to the common story, that he wanted to send the same liquor to all his generals. Apparently Lincoln never said it, but, when asked, he said it was a great quote and that he wished he had said it.

More officers and men were worried that Grant had come from the Western theater of the Civil War than about Grant's drinking. The last general to come from the West, John Pope, had arrived with a bang and left with a whimper after losing the Second Battle of Bull Run. More importantly, the soldiers reasoned, Grant had never faced Confederate generals as good as Robert E. Lee, the best the Confederates had.

Others, however, knew what to expect from Grant. James Longstreet, Lee's senior corps commander, warned his men not to underestimate

Grant. Longstreet, an old friend, pointed out that Grant had the persistence Meade lacked and said about Grant, "That man will fight us every day and every hour until the end of the war."[14]

Much less likely ever to have been said, but equally interesting on its face, is the supposed statement of Richard Ewell, back at the start of the Civil War. "There is one West Pointer, I think in Missouri, little known, and whom I hope the Northern people will not find out. I mean Sam Grant. I knew him well at the Academy and in Mexico. I should fear him more than any of their officers I have yet heard of. He is not a man of genius, but he is clear-headed, quick and daring."[15] A 1998 biography of Ewell[16] points out that Grant and Ewell had met but did not know each other well. At the beginning of the war, it is unlikely that Ewell made such a statement.

A few months after the April 1865 end of active campaigning in Virginia, Ulysses S. Grant submitted his report to the secretary of war on the last year of the Civil War. He showed a good understanding of the strategic and operational realities he had faced a year earlier.

> From an early period in the rebellion I had been impressed with the idea that active and continuous operations of all the troops that could be brought into the field, regardless of season and weather, were necessary to a speedy termination of the war. The resources of the enemy and his numerical strength were far inferior to ours; but as an offset to this, we had a vast territory, with a population hostile to the Government, to garrison, and long lines of river and railroad communications to protect, to enable us to supply the operating armies.
>
> The armies in the East and West acted independently and without concert, like a balky team, no two ever pulling together, enabling the enemy to use to great advantage his interior lines of communication for transporting troops from east to west, re-enforcing the army most vigorously pressed, and to furlough large numbers, during seasons of inactivity on our part, to go to their homes and do the work of producing for the support of their armies. It was a question whether our numerical strength and resources were not more than balanced by these disadvantages and the enemy's superior position.
>
> From the first, I was firm in the conviction that no peace could be had that would be stable and conducive to the happiness of the people, both North and South, until the military power of the rebellion was entirely broken. I therefore determined, first, to use the greatest number of troops practicable against the armed force of the enemy, preventing him from using the same force at different seasons against first one and then another of our armies, and the possibility of repose for refitting and producing necessary supplies for carrying on resistance; second, to hammer continuously against the armed

force of the enemy and his resources, until by mere attrition, if in no other way, there should be nothing left to him but an equal submission with the loyal section of our common country to the constitution and laws of the land. . . . All I can say is, that what I have done has been done conscientiously, to the best of my ability, and in what I conceived to be for the best interests of the whole country.[17]

Grant had to work in a political as well as a military context, as described by a historian: "Never before was the link between what was happening on the battlefield and what the public believed was happening so critical as in the spring of 1864. . . . How the public perceived the course of military operations and the prospects for success would determine the outcome at the polls in November."[18] Grant not only had to advance. He had to be seen to be advancing.

Grant had the major consideration of where he personally should be based. Grant quickly decided that the political pressures of locating in Washington itself would make his job substantially harder. These same pressures, however, and Robert E. Lee's presence in the East, made it necessary for Grant to locate in the East. William T. Sherman took over Grant's old job as overall "theater" commander in the West. Grant finally decided he would accompany the Army of the Potomac to be on the scene for the direct face off with Lee. Grant wanted to avoid the easy political interference that might occur were he accessible in Washington, but he thought he had to be near the capital. He also wanted to protect the Army of the Potomac from political interference.

Traveling with the Army of the Potomac would enable Grant to solve one odd command problem. Ambrose Burnside was back with the Army of the Potomac, in command of the IX Corps. Burnside was senior to Meade, by date of rank, so he could not come under Meade's command. Grant had to coordinate the moves of the Army of the Potomac with the IX Corps. (Burnside later agreed to serve under Meade.)

Andrew Atkinson Humphreys, chief of the staff of the Army of the Potomac, quotes Grant's aide Adam Badeau that "it was General Grant's duty himself to encounter [the inevitable political] difficulties, and to withstand, if he could not prevent, political interference; to remain where he could control all the movements of all the armies, absolutely and independently. . . . Unless he was near the capital, he could not control all the operations of all the armies without interruption. . . . In Washington General Grant would not stay in time of war; he must then direct, in person, the campaigns of that renowned Army of the Potomac."[19] Meade would remain in actual command of the Army of the Potomac.

Grant had to travel back and forth between his field headquarters and Washington in the weeks before the spring campaign began. One return trip from Washington could have been history making. Just before the train reached Warrenton Junction, about two-thirds of the way back to Grant's headquarters, a heavy cloud of dust was seen not far to the east of the railroad. Stopping the train at Warrenton, Grant asked what had happened. He was told that Confederate ranger John Mosby and some of his men crossed the line a few minutes before in pursuit of Federal cavalry. Grant wrote in his memoirs that had Mosby "see our train coming, no doubt he would have let his prisoners escape to capture the train."[20]

The North had not secured its victory when Grant took over. The Confederates were not convinced, as we may be today, that by the start of Grant's spring 1864 campaign the war was effectively over. Confederates, particularly those in his Army of Northern Virginia, still trusted Lee, and thought that under his command they could defeat Grant as they had defeated all the other Federal commanders who had invaded Virginia. The war may have been the North's to lose, but the North could still lose. Grant's actions in the coming campaign would make a difference.

As late as February 1864, Lee was still thinking of taking the offensive, but on a smaller scale than in the Gettysburg campaign the summer before.

> The approach of spring causes me to consider with anxiety the probable action of the enemy, and the possible operations of ours in the ensuing campaign. If we could take the initiative and fall upon them unexpectedly we might derange their plans and embarrass them the whole summer. . . . We are not in a condition . . . to invade the enemy's country with a prospect of permanent benefit. We can alarm and embarrass him to some extent, and thus prevent his undertaking anything of magnitude against us.[21]

Lee knew the danger of losing what initiative he had. He told Major General Jubal Early, "We must destroy this army of Grant's before he gets to [the] James River. If he gets there, it will become a siege, and then it will be a mere question of time."[22]

Grant favored what his end of the war report, quoted above, called "active and continuous operations of all the troops that could be brought into the field." He looked to the campaign, and coordination on different fronts, rather than particularly to a battle. But battles would have to be fought. One final decisive battle, though still unlikely at this point of the war, was possible.

Grant's Overland Campaign, the stab at Lee and Richmond by the Army of the Potomac, with cooperating efforts by Franz Sigel and a force in the Shenandoah Valley, and Benjamin Butler's Army of the James roughly duplicating McClellan's advance in 1862, were the key parts of the campaign in the East. In the West, Sherman would advance on Atlanta and Joseph Johnston's Army of Tennessee. A third major Federal effort, in Louisiana, would be under the command of Nathaniel P. Banks.

Grant had originally considered landing an army on the Atlantic Coast, between Richmond and North Carolina, and advancing on Richmond from that direction. This idea was rejected for its excess complexity, and the fact that the army would not also be able to meet Lincoln's basic requirement that Washington be covered. The more conventional three-pronged advance was the result.

Meade's Army of the Potomac was the main "force of maneuver." On April 9, 1864, Grant sent Meade overall strategic orders for the coming campaign. Two sentences stand out. "So far as practicable, all the armies are to move together and toward one common center. . . . Lee's army will be your objective point. Wherever Lee goes, there you will go also."[23]

General Andrew A. Humphreys, as chief of staff of the Army of the Potomac, designed the plan that Grant and Meade finally adopted. Ruling out a direct attack on Lee, in the very strong Confederate positions to the west at Mine Run, the Federals could go to their left or right flank.

Humphreys later wrote of the main arguments for and against each approach. He first pointed out that moving by the Federal right flank, against Lee's left, "would take us through a more open and cultivated country than that we should find in moving by our left,"[24] but it would require detaching increasing forces to protect the railroad and other supply lines. Humphreys pointed out the reality that "the proper care of the wounded, of which we expected to have a large number on hand in a few days, would be greatly facilitated by the easy access to water transportation that a movement by the left would afford."[25] The same open country that made Federal movement easier would let the Confederates observe the movements, and give them a day or two to get ready, including preparing "blocking positions" covering the roads.

A movement to the Federal left would enable the Federals to shorten their supply lines, and run the lines through areas the Federals more firmly controlled. However, General Humphreys, a veteran of the Battle of Chancellorsville, continued,

> The objection to moving by our left consisted in the character of the country south of the Rapidan . . . in which we might be obliged to fight our first

battle . . . the greater part of the country being covered with a forest, usually of dense growth, and over a large part of its extent there was . . . an almost impenetrable undergrowth, which it was very difficult for even small bodies of men to move in. To handle large bodies of troops in battle in such a field was exceedingly difficult. . . . an enemy remaining on the defensive awaiting attack where this undergrowth existed, would be unseen, while the troops advancing to attack would make their presence known.[26]

The main argument in favor of the Wilderness route was that if the army began moving early enough, it might be possible to get out of the heavily forested area, and at least partly turn Lee's right flank, before combat started. Humphreys said there was no question that the troops could do the required marching, as they had done so before, but, perhaps in retrospect, "the question was as to the practicability of moving the great trains of the army that distance simultaneously with the troops, so as to keep them under the cover of the army."[27] Though Grant would be willing to fight Lee when Lee attacked, Grant did not plan to fight in the Wilderness, where the difficulties of fighting on the heavily wooded area would negate Federal advantages in manpower and artillery. Grant's plan was not bad, if he could get his army through the forested area without being attacked.

Grant would take a reorganized Army of the Potomac into the Wilderness. A March 23, 1864, reorganization, planned by Meade, consolidated the five remaining corps into three. The I and III Corps were abolished, and their men distributed to the II, V, and VI. The XI Corps, under Oliver Otis Howard, and the XII, under Henry Slocum, had already been transferred to the West. John Newton of the I Corps, and William French of the III, both of whom had taken command during the Battle of Gettysburg, were sent west. Neither had served in corps command with much distinction.

George Sykes was removed from command of the V Corps, for reasons that were less clear. He was replaced by Gouverneur Kemble Warren. Winfield Scott Hancock returned to command the II Corps after recuperating from the serious wound he had received at Gettysburg. John Sedgwick remained in command of the VI Corps. The Federal cavalry got a new commander, the only change made at Grant's request. Alfred Pleasonton was replaced by Philip Sheridan, new to cavalry command.

A Federal private, assigned to an artillery company, was given some advice for the upcoming march. He was told to minimize his clothing. He was told to fill his canteen at every stream and at every opportunity. He was primarily told to "get hold of food, and hang on to it. You will need it."[28]

8

THE WILDERNESS

That man will fight us every day and every hour until the end of the war.

—James Longstreet, 1864[1]

Federal forces began to move out of camp just after midnight on May 4, 1864. By 6 a.m., Confederate pickets at the Rapidan River had been driven away by Federal cavalry, and the infantry was crossing. By 9 a.m., Confederate lookouts from a nearby elevated signal station had informed Lee that the spring campaign had started. Lee received different reports that day as to Federal intentions. He had to delay having his army move to meet the Federal advance since he was still not sure of the units' precise route.

About 11:15 that morning, Lee received a report from cavalry commander Jeb Stuart. Federal cavalry had been moving out in the direction of Confederate positions at Mine Run. The troops then suddenly withdrew. Stuart learned that a local resident had seen a courier ride up to Federal Brigadier General James Wilson, commanding the cavalry, with a dispatch ordering the advance to stop at "the church." Stuart presumed this meant the Wilderness Church, some four miles west of Chancellorsville. Stuart now realized, and reported, that Grant and Meade's army intended to swing around Lee's positions. Federal units were concentrated in the Wilderness and would likely take a good portion of the next day, May 5, to get out of the Wilderness.

Lee's three corps had the same commanders they had at Gettysburg, as did Lee's cavalry. The corps, under James Longstreet, Richard Ewell, and A. P. Hill, were far enough away that Lee did not try to contest Grant at the Rapidan, but instead planned to attack him in the Wilderness. When the Federal route became clearer, Ewell and Hill were ordered to head east, and Longstreet moved north, to the approximate area where Lee and Jackson had beaten Hooker a year before. When all forces were on hand, Lee would have sixty thousand men to resist Grant's one hundred thousand men, in the Army of the Potomac and the independent IX Corps under Ambrose Burnside. Lee wanted to fight Grant in the Wilderness itself, where Federal numbers and artillery would have much less of an advantage.

One of the Federal generals in the Wilderness later wrote about that environment in which the Federals were trying to avoid pitched battle.

> As for the Wilderness, it was uneven, with woods, thickets, and ravines right and left. Tangled thickets of pine, scrub-oak, and cedar prevented our seeing the enemy, and prevented any one in command of a large force from determining accurately the position of the troops he was ordering to and fro. The appalling rattle of the musketry, the yells of the enemy, and the cheers of our own men were constantly in our ears. At times, our lines while firing could not see the array of the enemy, not fifty yards distant. After the battle was fairly begun, both sides were protected by log or earth breastworks.[2]

About noon on May 4, Grant and his staff crossed the Rapidan at Germanna Ford, the westernmost of the three crossing points used by his army. Grant was handed a dispatch telling him that Ewell's corps was spotted moving toward the advancing Federal army. Grant immediately sent word to Burnside, waiting with his corps roughly thirty miles away at Warrenton, to march immediately for Germanna Ford to join the rest of the army.

By midafternoon on May 4, with the leading elements of the II Corps almost out of the Wilderness to the south, the Federal army halted. Grant and Meade did not want the army to become separated from its supply and ammunition trains. These wagons would stretch an estimated sixty miles. For just about the first time in its history, the Army of the Potomac may have been moving too fast.

Federal camps that night were quiet, and nervous. Some soldiers found bones of casualties unburied from Chancellorsville, which was not good for morale. Pickets heard rumbling off to the west and guessed that this noise was Lee's army headed toward them. It was.

One Federal later wrote of being with some other Federals, trying to determine whether human remains were Federal or Confederate. A veteran of the Battle of Chancellorsville the year before spoke with them. The veteran did not cheer them up.

> This region is an awful place to fight in. The utmost extent of vision is about one hundred yards. Artillery cannot be used effectively. The wounded are liable to be burned to death. I am willing to take my chances of getting killed, but I dread to have a leg broken and then to be burned slowly; and these woods will surely be burned if we fight here. I hope we will get through this chapparal without fighting.[3]

The group of soldiers agreed that the veteran would not get his wish, and that Lee would likely attack Grant in the Wilderness. Enlisted men, grunts, may not have had the so-called big picture, but they had some idea of the realities of war above their level.

The Federal advance into the Wilderness headed southeast down the Brock Road, today's Route 613. This was the reverse of part of the course taken by Stonewall Jackson in flanking Hooker at the Battle of Chancellorsville. Gouverneur K. Warren's V Corps, in the middle of the Federal advance, had stationed Charles Griffin's division facing west when his advance started. The Federals had learned at least one lesson from Jackson's flank attack on Howard's unprepared XI Corps a year before. However, this meant that the Federal right flank was being guarded by infantry, not by more mobile cavalry.

Grant and Meade knew that Lee's army was somewhere to the west of the Army of the Potomac. Federal cavalry should have been patrolling to the west, both to find Lee and to give warning of his approach. But most Federal cavalry was elsewhere. Meade had reports of Stuart's Confederate cavalry to the Federal left. Meade, therefore, was using most of the cavalry to guard Federal supply wagons, on the army's left, with the army between them and the likely direction of Confederate attack. One of the three cavalry divisions, under James Wilson, was already south of the Orange Plank Road, out of range of the probable location of Lee's first attack. The few Federal cavalrymen on the Orange Turnpike were not there long enough to spot and warn of the approaching Confederates.

Hancock was ordered to hold the II Corps in position just south of the Wilderness. Hancock's corps was eventually pulled back deeper into the Wilderness, to guard a key crossroads and maintain contact with the other Federal corps.

One thing that would become clear about this fighting was that tactically, best described as either the lower level of combat or combat on the immediate front lines, the battle was confused and even today is hard to follow.

Operations, the coordination of independent units, were more comprehensible. However, the operational art, as it is sometimes called, was not well developed at the time. Commanders on both sides would have problems coordinating movements of units outside of their immediate range of vision. Civil War units, even marching infantry, could frequently move faster than telegraphic communications could keep up. Federal forces had encountered problems at Chancellorsville in the delivery of telegraphic orders.

Saunders Field was not the only battle area that day in the Wilderness, but it was one of the central areas on May 5, the first day of the Battle of the Wilderness. Saunders Field was a cleared area, one of the few in the Wilderness, through which ran the Orange Turnpike, one of the few east/west roads through the Wilderness. (The field and the road still exist today.) Maps indicate a field roughly eight hundred yards in length, about four hundred yards wide, though the width varied. Most significantly, about the middle of the field there was a deep gully that could only be crossed on a small footbridge. With the need for an attacking force, going in either direction, to channel across the footbridge, Saunders Field was a good defensive position.

About 7 a.m., Warren responded to reports of Rebels in the area by sending skirmishers to the west to ascertain how close the Confederates had come during the night. When they came to Saunders Field, the bulk of Griffin's men still to the east, they noticed sizable numbers of Southern soldiers at the other end of the field, going into position in the woods and preparing earthworks. Warren had been preparing a note to Meade that he faced small numbers of Confederates to the west, but he was not planning on stopping the movement of his corps. Griffin was told to hold his ground facing west, and to be prepared to attack, though an attack was not yet ordered.

Warren added to his note to Meade a comment that the Confederates were there in force. When Meade received this message, he was already on his way to talk with Warren. Meade then suspended the army's movement for the day, and ordered Warren to attack the Confederate forces along the turnpike. Interestingly, at this point Meade notified Grant that Lee was trying to delay the Army of the Potomac's moving out of the Wilderness. This was an accurate conclusion, but by stopping the army and turning to give battle, Meade was inadvertently giving Lee battle where Lee wanted to fight.

Meade sent word to Grant that he was stopping the movement of the army until Griffin could find out the strength of the Confederates in his immediate front. Grant was pleased. He sent word back to Meade that "if any opportunity presents itself of pitching into a part of Lee's army, do so without giving time for disposition."[4] Grant wrote in his memoirs, about twenty years later, "It was my plan then, as it was on all other occasions, to

take the initiative whenever the enemy could be drawn from his intrenchments if we were not intrenched ourselves."[5]

Unfortunately, as a modern historian has pointed out, "Time for disposition, however, was precisely what Meade needed."[6] At least at this moment,
the Army of the Potomac may have been compensating for its previous
habit of slowness by attacking too quickly. Griffin's division was the only
one of Warren's divisions on the potential battle line. Sedgwick's corps,
which would guard Warren's right in an attack facing west, was too far away
to be of any help for several hours. Warren's other three divisions were
closer, but still not within supporting distance. Warren had no idea how far
Ewell's corps, the Confederates he was facing, extended into the woods on
either side of the visible defenses. The woods were too thick to try the same
trick he had tried at Little Round Top, to fire artillery shells into woods that
might contain troops and see what happened. The artillery would have to
be visible before it could fire, and within range of Confederate fire. Even if
the crews were not shot, the Confederates would have time to alert hidden
men to try not to react.

The contrast here with Hooker a year earlier is that though Meade also
stopped his army's movement in the Wilderness, Meade was preparing to
attack while Hooker was awaiting attack. Meade may have learned the lesson
from Hooker that it is very bad to surrender the initiative to Robert E. Lee.[7]

Interestingly, though Lee intended to attack Grant within the Wilderness, Ewell had been ordered not to bring on a general engagement until
the corps under A. P. Hill and James Longstreet arrived. Hill was close, but
Longstreet was not expected until late that afternoon.

Despite this, both sides were building up forces near Saunders Field.
One Federal soldier later remembered, "Here were two great armies, forming lines of battle for a desperate struggle, within half a mile of each other,
scarcely a movement of either of which could be observed by the other."[8]

About 7:30 a.m., a second message went from Meade to Warren, telling
Warren that help, in the form of the VI Corps, was on the way and to attack
as soon as possible. By 9:00 a.m., however, Meade was reporting to Grant
that Warren was making dispositions, getting ready to attack.

Meade did not know it, but in some ways he was operating as blind as
Hooker at Chancellorsville, or Lee at the start of the Battle of Gettysburg.
Though most Federal cavalry was in the area, not off raiding in the direction
of Richmond, two of the three cavalry divisions were on the Army of the
Potomac's left, protecting against an apparent, though unreal, threat from
Stuart's cavalry in that area. Meade was not getting reports from the third

cavalry division, on the side of his army facing Lee, under James Wilson. Wilson, operating somewhere to the south, had sent his last report at 5 a.m.

Meade's problem was one of information, particularly real-time information on current enemy movements. Federal military intelligence had detected Confederate movement on May 4, but could not know whether this would continue. Finding out was the job of Federal cavalry. Meade made some bad decisions at the start that made the job harder. One of three cavalry divisions was kept near Chancellorsville, on the left flank of the advance when danger would likely come on the right flank. A second division was moved there not long after the advance started. Only Wilson's division was patrolling the right flank of the army's advance, the side facing Lee, and his division soon moved too far to the south.

Meade was learning about Confederate movements, first on the Orange Turnpike, then a few miles to the south on the Orange Plank Road, from infantry commanders unpleasantly surprised by advancing Southerners.

Meade had ordered Wilson to patrol out the Orange Turnpike the morning of May 5. Meade intended Wilson to leave pickets on the turnpike. Wilson thought he was only to patrol and keep men there until Warren's infantry showed up. At the time Meade was not hearing from Wilson, Wilson's cavalry was engaged in combat with Confederate cavalry on the Catharpin Road, about six miles to the south of the Orange Turnpike. Wilson's men were pushed back in this engagement. They also found direct communication with Meade cut off by the advance of Hill's Confederate corps on the Orange Plank Road.

By 10 a.m., Warren had still not started his attack, and Meade still had no word from Wilson. Meade did learn that a second large Confederate force was advancing on the Orange Plank Road. Confederates were actually closer to the crossroads of the Orange Plank Road and the Brock Road than Federal forces. The Brock Road was the primary means of communications between Winfield Scott Hancock and the II Corps, just to the south of the Wilderness, and the rest of the Army of the Potomac. Losing control of this crossroads would cut Meade's army in two. Reinforcements had also not arrived as expected.

Meade seems to have planned his dispositions to meet a Confederate diversionary force. He now appeared to be facing, with an ill-planned and improvised deployment, Lee's entire army.

The Union forces were also missing an opportunity along the Orange Plank Road. The road was clear to the Brock Road. But one of Warren's divisions, under Samuel Crawford, was entering an area known as the Chewing Farm, about half a mile to the north. Crawford failed to reinforce a cavalry regiment holding the road, and he failed to immediately attack the Confederate flank. Crawford was not a particularly aggressive commander, and knew he could not get reinforcements. Crawford actually did not give up considering an attack until he received orders from Warren directing him to withdraw to the north to reinforce James Wadsworth's division, just south of Griffin's division. Even at this point, he stayed where he was, and sent word of the advance of Hill's corps.

At this early point in the battle, some odd patterns were emerging in Federal leadership. One was stopping the Army of the Potomac in the Wilderness the night of May 4 to allow the supply trains to catch up. Arguably, this idea had advantages, since though Meade did not know exactly where Lee was, Lee was not that far away and might have endangered the trains. However, an alternative explanation is that Meade was falling back into the Army of the Potomac's habit of taking things a little too leisurely.

Lee was also not having things go quite as he had initially intended. Lee's plan was not to start a full-scale battle until Longstreet came up, hopefully late in the afternoon of May 5. Ewell and Hill were supposed to pin the Federals in place until Longstreet could attack. This is not what happened.

Warren had received orders from Meade at 7:15 in the morning to attack Ewell with his whole force. General Sedgwick, with Wright's division and Neill's brigade of Getty's division, was ordered to move out, west of the Germanna Plank road, and connect with the V Corps across the Orange Turnpike. Winfield Scott Hancock, at his headquarters near the remains of the Chancellor House (even today still called Chancellorsville), received Meade's orders to halt his corps just south of the Wilderness, at Todd's Tavern.

A midmorning probe found Confederate troops quite close. For nearly four hours, however, Warren's corps experienced difficulty getting into position in the thick woods. At one point, Warren tried to get Meade to call off the attack, but Meade insisted the attack go forward. Sedgwick's corps was having trouble linking with Griffin's division, on Warren's right. On Griffin's left, a half-mile gap appeared between his and Wadsworth's division. Wadsworth was shifted, north, creating a gap with Crawford's division. Ewell's entire Confederate corps had gotten into position, and begun to entrench, during this delay in the Federal attack.

Warren finally attacked about 1:30 p.m. some six hours after first being ordered to attack. He was using two divisions, instead of the two corps Meade had initially planned to send into battle, so arguably the attack was little better off than had it been made when first ordered, with one division but against fewer Confederates. Attacking fixed positions was always highly dangerous in the American Civil War. For most of the war the defense was predominant. In fact, with odds anywhere near equal, it was extremely difficult, though not impossible, to dislodge a defender with a frontal assault.

Attacking through the Wilderness was more than just a dangerous walk. Running was virtually impossible in the underbrush, so covering the ground more quickly was not an option. The trees and brush sharply limited visibility. What visibility was left would have soon vanished as the black smoke of the period created heavy ground-level fog. Bullets would come from an unseen enemy. Defenders would have the same visibility problems, but a far greater chance of hearing the attacker in the smoke, and being able to shoot by sound.

Much of an attacker's power at the time came from concentrating fire and force, with the price of being a more concentrated target. But in the Wilderness units would lose alignment. At one point at the Battle of Chancellorsville, attacking Federal and Confederate columns had actually gone past each other's flanks without realizing what they had done. Units fired into their own men. (These disastrous accidents were not yet known as "friendly fire.") Other units wandered into enemy lines, being captured in one mass.

Clearings would not have come as a relief. As during the Battle of Chancellorsville, fought in virtually the same area, advancing troops were now, if briefly, visible and made far better targets to the defenders. Federal blue uniforms would have stood out much better against the trees than gray and butternut Confederate uniforms. However, Warren's attack had some initial success. On the Federal right Johnson's division of Ewell's corps was driven back along the Orange Turnpike in confusion by Griffin's division. The VI Corps divisions under brigadier generals Horatio Wright and James B. Ricketts were delayed in reaching their position on the right of Warren, and for lack of such support Griffin's right brigade under Brigadier General Romeyn B. Ayres was forced back and two cannons were abandoned.

Just south of the Orange Turnpike, Brigadier General Joseph J. Bartlett's brigade, attacking the same time as Ayres, also enjoyed some initial success. Elements of the 20th Maine, of Gettysburg fame, had a particularly interesting time during the battle. Colonel Joshua Chamberlain, and the regiment's second in command, were both in Washington, D.C., on court-martial duty, so the regiment was commanded by Major Ellis Spear. Holman Melcher was temporarily in command of Company F. He later wrote of his experiences,[9] providing an interesting "boots on the ground" perspective on the battle. Melcher begins with the customary remarks about the difficult environment the Wilderness area presented for both movement and combat.

"The night was quiet and restful after our long forced march"[10] on May 4. Bugles woke them up early the next morning, to prepare to advance to the west. (Melcher says nothing about whether using bugles to blow reveille was a good idea, if the sound might not carry to any nearby Confederate troops.) As the men of Bartlett's brigade were getting ready to advance west, the few cavalry scouts out in that direction came galloping back with word that Confederates were only about two miles away. "Affairs changed very suddenly; arms were stacked, shovels and picks brought up, and every man worked with a right good will to throw up earthworks [field fortifications] along the line . . . which was on a slightly wooded crest of a ridge running across the road."

Melcher says his men hoped for an attack, against their strong positions, which they were sure they could fight off. But an attack was ordered, and the unit moved out sometime around 1 p.m. on May 5. The 20th Maine was in the second line of attack of Bartlett's brigade. Melcher continues "climbing over the line of works we had erected with so much interest and pleasure, we pushed out through the thick woods in our front . . . till we came near an open field [Saunders Field] where lines were being carefully formed." What Holman and his men, in the second line of battle, saw was not encouraging.

> We saw the first line of battle about half way across [Saunders Field], receiving a terribly fatal fire from an enemy in the woods on the farther side.
>
> This field was less than a quarter of a mile across, had been planted with corn the year before, and was now dry and dusty. We could see the spurts of dust started up all over the field by the bullets of the enemy, as they spattered on it like the big drops of a coming shower you have so often seen along a dusty road. But that was not the thing that troubled us. It was the dropping of our comrades from the charging line as they rushed across the fatal field . . . to the terrible storm of leaden hail, and we knew it would soon be our turn to run this fire.

General Bartlett, on his horse, ordered the 20th Maine and the 118th Pennsylvania to charge. The two regiments joined the first line of Bartlett's brigade in sweeping over the Confederate field entrenchments: "there, in the thicket of bushes and briers, with the groans of the dying, the shrieks of the wounded, the terrible roar of musketry and shouts of command and cheers of encouragement, we swept them before us like a whirlwind," scattering portions of Edward Johnson's and Robert Rodes's divisions.

Melcher does not mention hearing any artillery. Artillery played very little role in the Battle of the Wilderness. Field artillery did not have the range to fire from the few clearings at enemy targets several miles away. Indirect fire, at targets the gunners could not see, was not a developed art at the time. Anyway, gunners would have hesitated to fire unseen into such deep woods for fear of hitting their own men.

"The pursuit with my company and those immediately about me continued for about half a mile, until there were no rebels in our front to be seen or heard; and coming out into a little clearing, I thought it well to reform my line." Melcher ran into a problem. He, fifteen men of his company, and two others were cut off and isolated. They did not want to retreat, as "to go back seemed the way for cowards to move," but they did not see moving forward as realistic, either, with no idea as to the location of the rest of their regiment. While talking with his first sergeant, Ammi Smith, one of his men came up to them and told Melcher, "Lieutenant, come this way and let me show you something."

> Following him, he led me to the Orange [Turn] Pike and pointing back down that straight level road he said "See that!" I looked in the direction he pointed and saw that which froze the blood in my veins and made my heart almost cease beating for a time. Some half a mile down the road from where we had just charged . . . I could see a strong column of rebel infantry moving directly across the road in our rear, completely cutting us off from the direction we had come.

Melcher quickly guessed, accurately as he points out, that Ayres's brigade, to their right, had been repulsed in their attempt to advance. Bartlett's brigade was called back rather than let it be flanked and cut off. Melcher and his men, to the far left, had not gotten the word. Addressing his men, Melcher told them what was happening and then rather dramatically added, "I had rather die in the attempt to cut our way out, than be captured to rot in rebel prisons." His men supported him. But the time for speech making ended, and they had to get back to their lines.

Melcher tried to navigate a circular course, southeast and then northwest, to try to get around Confederate lines and back to the regiment's fortified positions across Saunders Field. Even today, there are patches of woods in the area where navigation is quite difficult, but Melcher seems to have gotten his directions correct. However, the Southern lines extended farther than he thought. They would have to fight their way through.

Melcher formed his eighteen men, including himself, into a "line of battle" (quotation in the original), and approached a Confederate sector from the rear, as quietly as possible. The Federals were unnoticed, as the Confederates were looking in the direction from which an attack was bound to come. About fifteen yards away, when Melcher thought they had been detected, each Federal picked a target and then opened fire. The Federals then charged, shouting and demanding the Confederates surrender.

> They were so astonished and terrified by this sudden and entirely unexpected attack and from this direction, that some of them promptly obeyed and threw down their arms and surrendered. The desperately brave fought us, hand to hand; the larger part fled in every direction through the woods.

Melcher writes that this engagement included the only time he ever saw anyone bayoneted in his entire wartime service. This was reflective of most veterans' experiences, as despite guesses before the Civil War that bayonet charges and combat would be important, and dramatic commands to "give them the bayonet," bayonets were more a psychological than a practical weapon.[11] Bayonet charges might be ordered, but would be likely either to rout the enemy or fail before soldiers could come to individual bayonet combat.

In this particular case, one of Melcher's men ordered a Southerner to drop his rifle and surrender. However, the Confederate brought the rifle to his shoulder and tried to fire. The trigger clicked, but the gun did not fire. The Federal sprang forward, stabbed the Confederate through the chest, pinned him to the ground, and remarked, "I'll teach you, old Reb, how to snap your gun in my face!"

The Federals took just a few minutes to cut a hole in the Southern line, and, as a bonus, they captured thirty-two prisoners. Two Federals were killed, three severely wounded, but the Federals were able to bring off the wounded. The rest of the nearby Confederate positions fired after the Federals, but not too strongly for fear of hitting their own men. When the prisoners noticed they outnumbered their captors, they began to slow down and seemed to be preparing to jump their captors. Melcher persuaded them not to try anything. He drew his revolver, still fully loaded as he had used his sword in the combat, and announced to the prisoners, "The first man who does not keep up in his place will be instantly shot."

A wounded Confederate captain, and another prisoner to take care of him, were turned over to another Federal regiment. The remaining thirty Confederates were turned over to divisional headquarters. Melcher and his men were received with some surprise and disbelief when they rejoined their regiment. One officer even implied to Melcher that he and his men had fled back to their original camp. Three days later, this officer was killed in combat.

Melcher did think, just after turning over the prisoners, to return to division headquarters and get a receipt. He had his proof that his story was accurate.

Just to the south of Griffin's division, action was also underway. Wadsworth, with his division of Warren's corps, supplemented by Dennison's brigade of Robinson's division of the same corps, had started forward in a westerly direction, until he found himself with his left toward the enemy. McCandless's brigade of Crawford's division (also of Warren's corps) had endeavored to obtain a position on the left of Wadsworth, but lost its bearings in the entangled woods so that its left came in contact with Ewell's right, as well as Wadsworth's left flank being driven in by two Confederate brigades on Ewell's right.

Crawford now had his left flank "in the air," unprotected. His division was then drawn back slightly, shifted to face southwest. Wadsworth finally took position on the left of Crawford, facing toward the south and west, with his back toward the Lacy house. Griffin, on Crawford's right, reached to the Orange Turnpike. Wright's division of Sedgwick formed on the right of Griffin. The entire Union front line was now entrenched. At this time on the center and right Warren and Sedgwick were blocked by Ewell's corps.

About 11 a.m., Hancock was informed that enemy forces, Hill's corps, were coming down the Orange Plank Road in full force. Hancock was told that Getty's division had been sent to the key Brock/Orange Plank crossroads to delay Hill. Getty would need assistance as soon as possible. Hancock would have to move southwest on the Plank road to link up with Warren.

Getty did well, in fierce fighting forcing Hill's corps to stop its advance just short of the key crossroads. Even with the masterful Federal bluff—Getty's resistance trying to convince the Confederates that more than a Federal division was on hand—Hancock's arrival was timely. However, Hancock also faced the problem of coordinating his attack in the thick woods, including communicating with his division commanders and with Meade. Attacks would ideally maneuver over fronts a mile or more wide. Even today, with the Battlefield Park area, the Orange Plank Road measures maybe thirty feet wide. (Walking along the road, with no shoulder, when a car comes along the walker has to literally step into the woods.)

Hill's attack had suffered from the same problems as Hancock's. Harry Heth's division, the same one that had opened the fighting at Gettysburg, had led the Confederate assault down the Plank Road. Cadmus Wilcox's division was pretty much stuck behind Heth, until Hill decided to deploy the division into the woods to the north. The net result of the deployment problems was that Getty's division alone hit Heth's division alone, with both sides having problems bringing additional men into the fight.

One incident, interesting as it occurred, portentous in what might have occurred, took place just after noon on May 5 at the Tapp Farm, one of the largest clearings in the Wilderness area. Robert E. Lee, A. P. Hill, and Jeb Stuart were conferring at one end of a field when a Union company entered the other side of the field, about 150 yards away. The generals quickly headed to their horses and left the area. The Confederates were astute enough not to fire on the Federals and thus call attention to the valuable targets. The Union officer failed to recognize his chance to deal a crippling or fatal blow to the Army of Northern Virginia, if not to the entire Confederate war effort, and quickly withdrew his men. This "near death/ capture" experience played a major role in convincing Lee that Hill had to link up with Ewell, starting with extending Wilcox's division to the north of the Orange Plank Road.

A few hours later, under attack by Getty and the Federal II Corps, Hill's men fell back under the increasingly heavy pressure, but by the time darkness ended the fighting, they had not been routed. Poor visibility might have prevented a Confederate disaster. Hancock, back at the crossroads, had no way of knowing how his attack was going. A steady stream of wounded men coming to the rear did not help convince the Federals that their attack was going well.

Hill's men were not ordered to entrench that night. Hancock, on the other hand, had taken the precaution of ordering his men to build several lines of earthworks before moving to the attack.

The night could be horrible. The authors of the guide to Grant's overland campaign staff rides, prepared as background for military officers studying the campaign, describe what it was like:

> The night was horrible for both sides while they planned for the next day's battle. Fires started in the dry timber, and the flames often crept up to the wounded—many of whom could not move. Many suffocated or burned to death. Some of the wounded suffered even more when their cartridges were set off by the heat and exploded beside their bodies. Many soldiers, both North and South, remember this as one of the worst nights of the war.[12]

Other stories tell of the wounded calling for help, but with the cries stopping just before the cartridge boxes exploded. These may have been the lucky wounded, killed, or rendered unconscious, before the flames reached them.

The battle would have to continue the next day. Grant ordered Hancock to resume the attack at 5 a.m. Grant assumed Hancock could complete the major Federal victory he had been on the verge of accomplishing the day before. The other Federal units, including Burnside's corps that had now arrived, were to keep the pressure on all parts of the front, to keep Lee from reinforcing Hill, and to take advantage of any favorable development.

Fighting on May 6 actually started on the Federal right, with both Confederate probes and a Federal diversion effort. Hancock's attack, west on the Orange Plank Road, with a supporting attack by Wadsworth's division through the woods, started very well, aided by the fact that Hill's men had not entrenched. However, Burnside was slow in coming to Hancock's support. "Just what I expected,"[13] Hancock yelled when told of the delay.

The Federal attack was not achieving the quick and decisive results Grant had wanted. The Staff Ride Handbook authors speculate that part of the problem might have been that most of Hancock's attacking forces were on the road.[14] In the environment of the Wilderness, this would have made the attacking force easier to control. Hancock probably had a point. Even Jackson's smashing of Howard's right flank the evening of the second day at Chancellorsville ran into control problems after a few hours. However, Hancock was only gradually able to apply force on a limited area.

Still, just over an hour after fighting started, Hill was in deep trouble. Federal forces were approaching Tapp Farm, the scene of Lee's near personal disaster the day before. Then Longstreet's corps started to arrive.

Southern artillery went into position on the west side of Tapp Farm, one of the few places in the Wilderness where artillery could be used to any effect. A few volleys delayed the Federal advance. The first infantry to arrive, the division under Brigadier General Joseph Kershaw, deployed south of the road. One of Major General Charles Field's brigades joined Kershaw, but the others went to the north. The lead brigade here was the brigade of Texans, with one Arkansas regiment, under Brigadier General John Gregg. Though Confederate divisions and brigades were named after their current commanders, there were two exceptions. The Stonewall Brigade bore that name officially in honor of its first commander, Stonewall Jackson. The Texas Brigade was often called Hood's Brigade, in honor of its second and most famous commander, John Bell Hood.

Hood's Texas Brigade was ordered to charge Federal positions a few hundred yards away at the other end of Tapp Farm's field. As they were forming for the charge, Robert E. Lee rode up to their commander and asked what troops they were. When told the Texas Brigade, Lee reportedly replied, "I am glad to see it."[15] A few minutes later, after hearing Gregg address his men just before the attack, Lee was heard to say, "Texans always move them!"[16] Cheers followed as word of this spread through the brigade. Then things got interesting.

The men began to head toward the enemy. After they had gone some distance in the charge, the men noticed Lee was with them. Cries of "General Lee to the rear," "We won't move until you go back," and "Go back, General Lee, go back" were heard. Finally one man grabbed the saddle of Lee's horse to stop him from moving forward. The most likely candidate to have done this, according to historian Harold B. Simpson, was a Texas soldier named Leonard Groce Gee.[17] Finally General Gregg, assisted by Lee's aide Colonel Charles Veneble, persuaded Lee to go to a more appropriate place for the army commander, to join General Longstreet on a small knoll on the west side of the farm. Lee's brain had told him the day before to leave Tapp Farm's field when the Federal troops had appeared. Lee's emotions almost got the better of him that morning.

The Texans' attack, and a second attack by a Georgia brigade, were not decisive but succeeded in delaying the Federals and buying time for the Confederates. Several other Confederate probes finally stopped the Federals.

Grant and Meade had trouble sorting out their men and renewing the Federal offensive. The Southern efforts were more successful. Longstreet sent the army's chief engineer, Major General Martin L. Smith, to search for any openings on the Federal left, southern, flank. Smith found a railroad bed, where the tracks had not been laid, south of the Union lines. The Federals did not seem to know about the cut. Confederate forces could move unnoticed around the Federal flank and deploy unseen on flatter ground. This is what they did, throwing back the Federal left. After the war Hancock told Longstreet, "You rolled me up like a wet blanket, and it was some hours before I could reorganize for battle."[18]

About two hours later, Longstreet was riding with some staff members and subordinate commanders. Brigadier General Micah Jenkins had just finished expressing renewed confidence in the Confederate cause when a volley of gunfire erupted from nearby woods. Two staff officers were killed immediately. Jenkins was mortally wounded with a bullet in the head. Most seriously for the Confederate cause, another bullet passed through Longstreet's neck and into his right shoulder, paralyzing his right arm. Longstreet was out of action for five months. Joseph Kershaw, a division commander riding with Longstreet, quickly determined that this was "friendly fire" from a Confederate unit that had mistaken Jenkins's nearby brigade for Federals. Kershaw managed to stop the units from firing on each other. Longstreet was accidentally shot by his own men just a few miles from where, a year before under similar circumstances, Jackson had been accidentally shot by his own men.

With Longstreet out of action, Lee took personal command of Longstreet's men. By the time Lee was able to get his attack started, changing direction from Longstreet's attack, darkness made it impossible to produce more than an orderly Federal withdraw to the entrenchments at the Brock/ Orange Plank crossroads. The remaining heavy fighting, on the Federal right, was scary but indecisive.

Grant's headquarters was receiving reports that Sedgwick's VI Corps had been routed, or even virtually destroyed. At one point an officer rushed up to Grant and warned, "General Grant, this is a crisis that cannot be looked upon too seriously. I know Lee's methods well by past experience; he will throw his own army between us and the Rapidan, and cut us off completely from our communications." Grant responded, apparently heatedly, unusual for Grant, "Oh, I am heartily tired of hearing about what Lee is going to do. Some of you seem to think he is suddenly going to turn a double somersault, and land in our rear and on both of our flanks at the same time. Go back to your command and try to think what we are going to do, instead of what Lee is going to do."[19]

Little fighting took place on May 7, as both sides entrenched in anticipation of more fighting the next day. In the words of the Staff Ride Handbook, "Tactically the Confederates had proven skillful and exacted considerable Union casualties. By the end of 6 May, Lee had established a solid defensive line that discouraged further Federal attacks. Yet, the Northern forces were not defeated. From an operational perspective, Grant and Meade had only fought their first battle of the campaign. Certainly, the Federals would have welcomed a clear victory, but with that result denied, the Union leadership planned its next move."[20]

On the night of May 7, 1864, the Army of the Potomac began to move out of the Wilderness. Grant's right flank led the movement, as the left held in position. The advanced element came to the Brock Road/Orange Plank Road crossroads. Turning left up the Orange Plank Road led back to Washington, the customary route for a defeated Federal army. The army then noticed that their generals were staying on the Brock Road, the road to Richmond. Grant described what happened next:

> With my staff and a small escort of cavalry I preceded the troops. Meade and his staff accompanied me. The greatest enthusiasm was manifest as we passed by. No doubt it was inspired by the fact that the movement was south. It indicated to them that they had passed through the "beginning of the end" in the battle just fought.[21]

9

TO PETERSBURG[1]

Active and continuous operations of all the troops that could be brought
into the field, regardless of season and weather, were necessary to a
speedy termination of the war.

—General Ulysses S. Grant, July 1865[2]

Jackson's attack the second day of the Battle of Chancellorsville, though it
smashed Hooker's right flank, did not end that battle. In the same manner,
vital as it was, Grant's heading south after the Battle of the Wilderness did
not end the war. Tipping points can require follow-up, and they can easily tip back if their effects are not monitored and future potential tipping
points not spotted and handled properly. Grant's persistence, and active and
continuous operations, would be required for many more months to come.

Lee detected Grant's move south. Rather than try to attack the Federals
remaining in their trenches, Lee ordered his men to head south themselves.
He guessed that the Federals were headed to Spotsylvania, less than ten miles
south of the Wilderness battlefield. The advanced Confederate units won the
race. They entrenched, and held off the first of a series of Federal attacks.

Entrenching had become popular during the fall campaigns in 1863, following the Battle of Gettysburg. "In the winter of 1863–1864 soldiers on
both sides of the American Civil War learned the value of temporary field
entrenchments. It did not result from any articulated shift in tactical doc-

trine, but rather seems to have emerged out of a spontaneous recognition by veteran troops that to dig was to survive."[3]

Entrenching fit in with the changed realities of the Civil War after Grant took over. His focus was on the campaign, rather than the battle, on his professional opinion that though it would be nice to get Lee to come out to fight one last decisive battle, it was more likely the Federals would probably have to use attrition to wear down Confederate strength to a point where they could no longer resist and the war would end. Such a straight-out war of attrition, seeing which side ran out of men and resources first, was un-winnable for the South. Lee knew his army was no longer strong enough for the wide-ranging strategic offensives of a year before. Local offensives, at targets of opportunity, would remain a Confederate tactic until the end of the war in the East.

Lee still had hopes of winning a war of nerves with the North. If Lee could prevent Grant from winning a major battle, perhaps the Northern population would decide the war could not be won. They might then force the Lincoln administration to make peace, or vote it out of office in the November 1864 presidential elections.

After the Battle of the Wilderness, when not engaged in a local attack, Lee's men would stay in their trenches. The Federals, remaining in contact with the Confederates, would have to dig and occupy their own trenches. Soldiers on both sides also learned that trenches could only rarely be taken by direct frontal attack, and then only by a particularly skilled attack. At Spotsylvania, on May 10 and May 12, the Federals nearly pulled off such attacks. In both cases they aimed at a bulge in the Confederate lines called the Mule Shoe. The attacking units stormed the trenches without taking time to fire, therefore spending far less time exposed to enemy fire. The Union forces did not use enough men in the first attack. Heavy forces were used for the second effort, two days later. However, the Confederates held off the attackers long enough to construct a second trench line at the base of the Mule Shoe.

From Spotsylvania, Grant had sent a telegram to Lincoln and Secretary of War Edwin Stanton stating that he would fight it out at that point if it took all summer. Lincoln's assistant, John Hay, noted in his diary for May 9, 1864, that "the President thinks highly of what Grant has done. He was talking about it today with me and said 'How near we have been to this thing today and failed. I believe that if any other General had been at the Head of the army it would have now been on this side of the Rapidan. It is dogged pertinacity of Grant that wins.' It is said that Meade observed to

Grant that the enemy seemed inclined to make a Kilkenny cat fight of the affair, & Grant answered, 'Our cat has the longest tail.'"[4]

The persistent Grant was willing to keep pressing Lee, when this was the best strategy. However, by May 20, Grant had ordered another move south, in an attempt to outflank Lee. Inconclusive fighting occurred at Hanover Junction and North Anna River a few days later. By May 30, the Federal army had moved to a point known as Cold Harbor. This seemingly odd name, for a place many miles from the ocean, came from the term for an inn where travelers could get shelter but not hot food.

The Cold Harbor attack was delayed from June 2 to June 3 since not all Federal forces had arrived in the area. This gave the Confederates extra time to prepare. Even worse, from the Federal point of view, was that the Confederate positions looked less strong then they were. In a battle lasting less than half an hour, the Federals lost roughly two thousand dead, five thousand wounded. For the time spent in actual fighting, the seven thousand Federal and fifteen hundred Confederate casualties make Cold Harbor the bloodiest period of fighting in the Civil War, surpassing any similar period in American history.

After Cold Harbor, Grant was four miles from Richmond but stalemated by seemingly impregnable Confederate positions. The armies had been in continuous contact for almost a month. Despite his reputation as a "butcher" unconcerned about casualties—Lee lost a higher percentage of his men in battle than Grant—Grant was a very flexible commander. Instead of a direct strike at Richmond, he decided to cut off the supply lines to both the Confederate capital and Lee's army. This could be done by moving south about twenty miles and taking the town of Petersburg, which controlled all but one rail line into Richmond.

Bruce Catton later wrote, "Never had the army been in a better strategic position than it was getting into this fifteenth of June."[5] Three days earlier, Federal forces quietly began to withdraw from Cold Harbor, Virginia, and head south, toward Petersburg, Virginia. The men took a route curving east, away from the Confederates, before turning and heading south. Lee anticipated a Federal move, probably continuing the Federal pattern of the last five weeks: trying to swing around the Federal right flank.

This time, however, Lee planned to do more than just ensure the temporary survival of his army, and his cause, by keeping in front of his enemy. Lee was going to try to catch Grant and the Army of the Potomac in motion. Lee hoped he would catch the Federals when they were most vulnerable, when they were crossing the Chickahominy River, north of Richmond, Virginia. Northern victory in the American Civil War was not yet inevitable.

Lee had the potential to score a major victory, and perhaps change the course of the war.

Grant's move caught Lee by such surprise that Lee went ahead with a planned diversion. On June 13, 1864, Lee sent Major General Jubal Early and the Second Corps northwest into the Shenandoah Valley to clear out Federal troops under David Hunter. When Hunter retreated into West Virginia, Early took his corps all the way to Washington, D.C. President Abraham Lincoln watched some of the fighting at Fort Stevens, early in July, on the outskirts of 1864 Washington—but well within the limits of the modern city.

By June 15 Lee had still not detected the Federal move. Advancing Federal troops from the XVIII Corps, cavalry, and "colored" units (African American soldiers with white officers) from a X Corps division were approaching Petersburg. The African American division had never seen combat, and had been stationed at City Point, the main Federal supply base on the James River. The XVIII Corps, under William F. "Baldy" Smith, had been borrowed from the Army of the James, Benjamin Butler's Federal army approaching Richmond and Petersburg from the East. Smith was in command of the entire force, at least until the expected arrival of the II Corps, under Winfield Scott Hancock, later that day.

At six o'clock that morning, Smith's force ran into Confederate resistance at a place called Baylor's Farm, several miles northeast of Petersburg. The Southerners held up the Federal advance for two hours.

Smith's men had arrived at Petersburg by about 2 p.m. Rather than immediately attack the Confederate positions, Smith decided to take a careful look. Despite evaluating the positions as strong but undermanned, Smith determined not to attack until he was fully ready. Two weeks before, Smith's men had been rushed to attack at Cold Harbor, and they were slaughtered. Smith did not wish to repeat this mistake, but, further motivated by the Confederate resistance at Baylor's Farm, he may have been overcautious—still a problem in the Army of the Potomac. However, when Smith's attack finally began at 7 p.m., it was quite successful. His man carried nearly a mile of trenches, including nine fortified positions known as "redoubts." By 9 p.m., Smith's first attack ended. He thought his troops were becoming disorganized, and he did not want to press his luck and did not attack further.

After a slow, daylong march most of June 15, Hancock was finally informed of the need to get to Petersburg quickly. He arrived about 9 p.m., just as Smith's first attack was ending. The Federals had over twice as many men in the area as the Confederates. However, rather than ordering an attack with the fresh and potentially overwhelming forces he now had, Smith did not act. He was satisfied just to ask Hancock to have his men take over the positions held by the XVIII Corps and the African American troops.

In his prime, Hancock, one of the more aggressive Federal generals, would have overruled Smith (Hancock was the senior general of the two) and attacked. But Hancock was not in his prime. He still had not fully recovered from a serious wound received a year earlier at the Battle of Gettysburg. The wound was causing Hancock a lot of pain and sapping his initiative. He deferred to Smith.

Hancock's men reacted unusually that night. Exhausted from six weeks of virtually constant fighting and very heavy casualties, one might have expected relief at being told to rest. However, they sensed that they had stolen a march on Lee and that a chance was at hand to end the war with one more attack. They may have been right. A common remark among men that night was, "Put us into it, Hancock, my boy, and we'll end this damned rebellion tonight."[6]

They were outraged when they learned no attack was to be made that night, when the odds would be far more in their favor than would be the case if they attacked a few days later, when Lee's army would arrive. One veteran later wrote, "The rage of the enlisted men was devilish. The most bloodcurdling blasphemy I ever listened to I heard that night, uttered by men who knew they were to be sacrificed on the morrow. The whole corps was furiously excited."[7]

General Pierre G. T. Beauregard, commanding the defenses of Petersburg, recognized the opportunity the Federals had that evening. After the war he wrote, "Petersburg at that hour was clearly at the mercy of the Federal commander, who had all but captured it, and only failed of final success because he could not realize the fact of the unparalleled disparity between the two contending forces."[8] Smith and Hancock seemed to be the only ones on the scene who did not recognize the Federal opportunity.

Beauregard asked Lee for reinforcements from Lee's army. Lee refused, as he did not consider the attacks on Petersburg to be Grant's main effort. Later that evening, Beauregard pulled one of his divisions from the lines blocking the Army of the James at the Bermuda Hundred peninsula. Beauregard now had about fourteen thousand men to try to hold the extensive Petersburg lines. He was still outnumbered, and the Bermuda Hundred defenses were far weaker, but time was running out for a quick Federal victory.

The Federals had another opportunity on June 16, 1864, the next day. Ambrose Burnside and his IX Corps arrived, giving the Federals substantially more men in the Petersburg area than the Confederates. However,

Federal attacks were not pushed with sufficient vigor and accomplished nothing. Another large chunk of Confederate trenches was taken on June 17. Once again, however, in the spirit of Smith's lack of aggression two days before, this success was not followed up.

The next day, Saturday, June 18, the Federals tried again—an early morning attack hitting empty trenches. Beauregard had pulled back, and it took the Federals some time to find his new positions.

Most of the Army of the Potomac was now on the scene. Lee's army was starting to arrive—Lee having finally recognized that Petersburg was Grant's main target—but the Federals still substantially outnumbered their enemy. George Meade, the actual commander of the Army of the Potomac and Grant's immediate subordinate,

> tried to coordinate a major attack at noon. He even went so far as to send his corps commanders instructions to telegraph his headquarters for the correct time, so the attacks might be simultaneous. This early effort at "synchronizing watches" was not successful. A recent historian has put it well in writing that "Somewhere in the strained machinery of the army, a gear wheel went askew, the various pieces of the Army of the Potomac and the Army of the James lurched piecemeal into battle, with Meade helpless to affect the course of events."[9]

The Army of the Potomac still needed continued persistence, and upper-level coordination, and even this did not always work. Records of the period show Meade telegraphing corps commanders strongly reminding them that his attack orders were explicit and that he wanted an immediate assault. The individual attacks failed, with heavy Federal casualties.

By the end of Saturday, June 18, sufficient troops from the Army of Northern Virginia had arrived to end the chance for a quick and easy Federal victory. That same day, Hancock, still suffering the effects of his wound at Gettysburg, temporarily turned over command of the II Corps to his ranking division commander, Major General David Birney, and went on medical leave. At Petersburg, and at Richmond twenty miles away, the siege had begun.

Patience was still needed as a major, if not the major, Federal war resource. The siege of Petersburg would be a long and slow process, for much of the time being little more than a stalemate. Worse, in a political war, it gave the impression of stalemate. The other three major Federal efforts also seemed to be getting nowhere. The Shenandoah Valley campaign, under Franz Sigel and then David Hunter, was making little progress—though not as disastrous for the Federal image as when Jackson made fools of his opponents. Jubal Early had been able to go through the Valley to get to Washington.

Nathaniel Banks, once known as "Jackson's commissary" for the amount of supplies he lost to Jackson, nearly lost his army in the Red River campaign in Louisiana. William Sherman could not seem to bring Joseph Johnston's army to grips in Tennessee and Georgia. This war of maneuver, though moving closer and closer to Atlanta, seemed to be getting nowhere. Benjamin Butler, commanding the Army of the James and meant to be supporting Grant, had managed to get himself bottled up on a small peninsula below Petersburg.

The situation seemed so stalemated that Lincoln wondered if he had any chance of winning reelection in 1864. In the third week of August, Lincoln asked his cabinet members to sign the outside of a memo they had not read. Dated August 23, 1864, the memo read: "This morning, as for some days past, it seems exceedingly probable that this Administration will not be reelected. Then it will be my duty to so co-operate with the President elect, as to save the Union between the election and the inauguration; as he will have secured his election on such ground that he cannot possibly save it afterwards."[10] Lincoln's success was as important to Grant as Grant's success was to Lincoln. What made things particularly galling is that George McClellan was the likely Democratic nominee for president.

When the Democratic convention met a few days later, McClellan was nominated. The interesting thing is that the Democratic platform was so antiwar that even McClellan, in his letter of acceptance, said the war should continue until it was won. The Democratic platform called for a negotiated settlement.

On September 3, 1864, Lincoln received a telegram from William Sherman that Atlanta had fallen. Admiral David Farragut had captured Mobile Bay a few days earlier. On September 19, 1864, Philip Sheridan, sent to ensure that the Shenandoah Valley would finally be closed as a Confederate invasion route, defeated Jubal Early's small army at Winchester. Lincoln no longer had to worry about staying in office.

10

END GAME[1]

Lieutenant-General Grant: Gen. Sheridan says, "If the thing is pressed,
I think Lee will surrender."
Let the thing be pressed.

—Abraham Lincoln to Ulysses S. Grant, April 7, 1865[2]

The siege of Petersburg had continued for nine months. The focus of
the action in the war had shifted to the West. Sherman pressed inexorably
through Georgia and South Carolina. A second major Federal force, under
George Thomas, badly defeated John Bell Hood's army at Franklin, and then
virtually destroyed that army a few weeks later at the Battle of Nashville.

In the end of March 1865, the center of action shifted back East. A Federal move around the Confederate right at Petersburg began on March 29,
1865. Philip Sheridan and the cavalry took a wide swing around the end of
Lee's lines and headed for Dinwiddie Court House. The V Corps took a
more direct route to the strategic White Oak Road. The II Corps, and the
troops from the Army of the James, extended the left of the Federal lines.

The first contact with Confederate resistance came that same day at a
place known as Lewis Farm, near the Quaker Road. The battle started at a
place called Gravely Run. Part of Bushrod Johnson's Confederate Division
was defending a position just across the shallow creek. The commander of
the V Corps's lead brigade, Joshua Lawrence Chamberlain, quickly brushed

aside Confederate opposition. Southern forces retreated back to their position at Lewis Road.

Chamberlain then attacked the Confederates at Lewis Road. He was
driven back, but he diverted the Confederates enough that Warren and
the rest of the V Corps could extend the Federal lines. Johnson's division
retreated at dusk, to White Oak Road. Warren's men now held the Boydton
Plank Road, one of Lee's last supply lines and Lee's only direct connection
with his maneuver force under George Pickett.

Sheridan's cavalry reached Dinwiddie Court House late on March 29.
Sheridan received instructions from Grant to head north to Five Forks, a
highly strategic road junction. Holding Five Forks, Sheridan would be able
to cut the two remaining railroads into Petersburg. Lee would then have to
evacuate Petersburg and Richmond. Sheridan sent a cavalry division to try
to take Five Forks that night. Pickett's forces held Five Forks, so the division withdrew slightly to the road from Dinwiddie to Five Forks.

The next day, March 30, heavy rains made a Federal advance all but impossible. On March 31 Sheridan and the cavalry would go after Five Forks.
G. K. Warren's V Corps would head for White Oak Road, to cut off the
route Lee needed to reinforce Pickett.

The Confederates opened the fighting that day. Infantry under Pickett
and cavalry under Fitz Lee attacked Sheridan from the west. Sheridan had
only four brigades in the immediate area of combat, and he was forced
back. Sheridan sent one message to Grant saying that he would likely be
forced back from Dinwiddie Court House. A second message, delivered
in person to Horace Porter, was more positive. Porter quoted Sheridan as
saying that he would hold Dinwiddie. Sheridan then added, referring to
Pickett, Fitz Lee, and their men, that "this force is in more danger than I
am. If I am cut off from the Army of the Potomac, it is cut off from Lee's
army, and not a man in it ought ever to be allowed to get back to Lee. We
have at least drawn the enemy's infantry out of its fortifications, and this is
our chance to attack it."[3]

The near simultaneous battle of White Oak Road proved Sheridan's
point. The V Corps had been advancing to Sheridan's right, but with no direct connection. In late morning Warren was attacked and forced back by a
smaller Confederate force. He managed to recover in the afternoon, pushing the Southern force back to its main White Oak Road line. Warren saw
that the line was too strong for an immediate attack. What mattered more,
though, is that Warren was now between Lee and his last maneuver force.

Grant and Sheridan could see that despite the apparent dangers to Sheridan's force, by using Warren's corps they could destroy Pickett. Implement-

ing this move, however, caused a series of sometimes confusing and contra-dictory orders to be sent to Warren. (Army of the Potomac communications problems were never solved.) Some orders arrived out of sequence. One particularly unfortunate message, from Grant to Sheridan, assured Sheridan that the V Corps would arrive about midnight. This was a realistic estimate only if the V Corps had already been assembled and ready to move. The corps, still in close contact with the enemy, was not ready to move.

The Federals made contact with some of Pickett's men. Pickett now knew the Federals were in his rear. He started to withdraw north, to Hatcher's Run. However, Lee ordered Pickett to hold Five Forks. Pickett placed his men in an L-shaped position along the White Oak Road, with the longer part facing south. Pickett's left, the short arm of the L, angled north-ward. The gap between Pickett's left and the nearest part of Lee's main line, under Anderson, was supposed to be covered by a small brigade under William P. Roberts, then the youngest general in the Confederate army.

Sheridan, never the most patient of men, was anxiously awaiting War-ren's arrival. Warren's corps did not arrive until morning. Warren was not at the head of the column—a general like Sheridan usually was. Warren was at the rear, personally supervising withdrawal from close contact with Confederate forces. When he finally did arrive, Warren delayed reporting to Sheridan for about three hours.

After further delays in V Corps's getting into position, the Federal attack did not start until 4:15 in the afternoon of April 1. The plan was to strike, hard, the angle where Pickett's line turned north. Unfortunately, Pickett was not where Sheridan and Warren thought. The V Corps headed off into empty space. The left of the V Corps, the division under Romain Ayres, started taking fire on its left flank. Ayres realized the problem, turned left, and attacked the Confederates. Samuel Crawford's division, on the right, kept going, opening a gap.

Charles Griffin, behind the other two divisions, moved to fill the gap. By 5:30 p.m., Ayres and Griffin had crushed Confederate defenses on the left. Warren was chasing after Crawford, whom he eventually found and turned around. Crawford's division hit Pickett in the rear, capturing a large number of prisoners and sending the rest retreating to the west, away from Lee's army. Crawford's initial error probably increased the scope of the Federal victory.

Unfortunately, Warren was dealing with Sheridan. Despite the clear Federal victory, Sheridan became angry when he could not find War-ren. Using authority given him by Grant, Sheridan relieved Warren and replaced him with Griffin. Sheridan was likely not being fair to Warren. However, as historian Bruce Catton later put it:

> This was the first time in the history of the Army of the Potomac that a rank-ing commander has been summarily fired because his men had been put into action tardily and inexpertly. Sheridan had been cruel and unjust—and if that cruel and unjust insistence on driving, aggressive promptness had been the rule in this army from the beginning, the war probably would have been won two years earlier.[4]

Lee's commanders in the area—Pickett, Fitz Lee, and Richard Anderson —fared worse than Warren. They were attending a shad bake behind the lines. The battle was virtually over by the time they knew anything was wrong.

About 9 p.m. on April 1, Grant learned of the great success. He now had forces behind Lee's lines. He ordered a general assault along all the Petersburg and Richmond lines. Breakthroughs occurred in several places, slicing up the Southern defenses. One was on the right of Lee's main lines, when the Federal Sixth Corps scored a notable success against A. P. Hill's Confederate Third Corps. Lee was at his headquarters, behind the lines in this area, conferring with Hill and First Corps Commander James Long-street when they learned of the Federal success. Hill left to try to repair the situation with his own corps. He and an aide saw two Federal soldiers and attempted to capture them. The Federals took shelter behind a tree, aimed their rifles, and fired. The one aiming at the aide missed. The other shot Hill through the heart. Hill was probably dead before he hit the ground.

Lee learned of Hill's death about the same time he realized the situation at Petersburg could not be repaired. The siege was over; Petersburg and Richmond would fall. A few hours later, while sitting in church, Jefferson Davis received a message from Lee, through the secretary of war, that Richmond would have to be evacuated that night. Lee's concern was now to save his army and then what to do with it.

J. R. Jones, in his diary, wrote of word "on the street" that day:

> A street rumor says there was bloody fighting yesterday a little beyond Pe-tersburg, near the South Side Road, in which Gen. Pickett's division met with fearful loss, being engaged with superior numbers. It is said the enemy's line of intrenchments was carried once or twice, but was retaken, and remained in their hands.
>
> I hear nothing of this at the [Confederate War] department; but the ab-sence of dispatches there is now interpreted as bad news! Certain it is, the

marching of veteran troops from the defenses of Richmond, and replacing them hurriedly with militia, can only indicate an emergency of alarming importance. A decisive struggle is probably at hand—and may possibly be in progress while I write. Or there may be nothing in it—more than a precautionary concentration to preserve our communications.[5]

Lee's army might not even last the day. Sheridan's victory at Five Forks had cut off that road for retreat. Lee's forces at Petersburg, forced back to a line of inner defense works created for such an emergency, would first have to retreat northward, over the few bridges over the Appomattox River, and then head west. The Federals would have to be held off until night. Despite heavy Federal attacks, the Confederates managed to hold until nightfall.

The Army of Northern Virginia, and the Confederate government, left Richmond that evening. The government headed southwest, the army almost directly west. Lee's intentions were to first get clear of Grant's closely pressing army, then reach supplies, particularly food, he had been told were waiting to the west at Amelia Court House. He then planned to swing south to try to hook up with Joseph Johnston's Confederate army in North Carolina, facing Sherman's army, now only about one hundred miles to the south of Richmond.

Law and order seemed to leave Richmond with the army and the government. The anarchy increased when the fires from strategic materials, ordered burned by Lee, and from burning government papers got out of control and spread. Frightened residents began to loot. A recent historian writes, "The once-defiant capital of the Confederacy was a hell of chaos, civilians and soldiers scurrying about, explosions and gunshots ripping the air, and the dust and smoke of a dying nation fogging the streets."[6]

A Confederate cavalry officer, in charge of one of the last units out of Richmond, later wrote about the evacuation of Richmond:

> The roaring and crackling of the burning houses, the trampling and snorting of our horses over the paved streets as we swept along, wild sounds of every description, while the rising sun came dimly through the cloud of smoke that hung like a pall around him, makes up a scene that beggars description, and which I hope never to see again—the saddest of many of the sad sights of war—a city undergoing pillage at the hands of its own mob, while the standards of an empire were taken from its capitol, and the tramp of a victorious enemy at its gates.[7]

A dramatic symbolic end to the siege of Richmond occurred on April 3. Richmond had a visitor—Abraham Lincoln. Accompanied by his son Tad,

Admiral David Porter, and at most a dozen sailors, after a short meeting with Grant at Petersburg, Lincoln had come to look at the now former Confederate capital. They arrived before most of the Federal troops were sent to occupy the city. Most white citizens stayed inside. Masses of black citizens came out, however, to see Lincoln. Lincoln's visit that day also included a trip to the Confederate White House, where he sat at Jefferson Davis's desk.

Grant, meanwhile, was busy pursuing Lee. He had decided the best way would not be to chase Lee, but to try to get in front of the Confederates. Lee was aiming toward Amelia Court House, to unite the five strands of his army and pick up promised supplies, primarily food. A second store of rations was waiting at Danville, further to the west. Lee and his men were in for an unpleasant shock on April 4, when they reached Amelia Court House. They found enough train cars, but they were filled with artillery equipment and ammunition. The nearby countryside was unable to help, having been stripped clean of food the winter before. With the Federals closing, Lee and the army would have to leave quickly.

On April 6, the Federal VI Corps and cavalry caught up to Confederate forces under Richard Ewell and Richard Anderson at Sayler's Creek. In a battle starting in the late afternoon, this section of Lee's army was virtually destroyed. Ewell himself and Lee's son General G. W. C. Lee were among the Confederate prisoners. The next day, despite the disaster, Lee politely rejected a message from Grant that the Confederate surrender.

The morning of April 9, Federal forces got ahead of Lee at a small hamlet called Appomattox Court House. At Lee's instructions, John Gordon's men staged one more attack. They brushed aside Federal cavalry, and then saw what was behind the cavalry and a small hill—three full-strength Federal infantry corps, outnumbering Lee's entire force. The rest of the Federal army was closing in on Lee from the east. The north was open, but the only option in that direction was for the army to disperse and try to fight as partisans. Lee rejected this option as promising just more bloodshed.

It took nearly four years from the firing on Fort Sumter for Richmond and Petersburg to fall to Federal forces—April 12, 1861, to April 2, 1865. One week later, at three o'clock in the afternoon of April 9, 1865, seventy-five miles to the west of Petersburg, at Appomattox Court House, Lee surrendered the Army of Northern Virginia to Ulysses S. Grant.

⓫

MEANING

We must genuinely be ready for the unexpected that is an inevitable part of our future.

—Colonel Thomas X. Hammes, USMC (ret.), 2004[1]

About a year after the end of the American Civil War, Grant formally reported on the last year of the campaign. Grant summarized his views two years earlier, when he had taken over command of all Federal armies: "From an early period in the rebellion I had been impressed with the idea that active and continuous operations of all the troops that could be brought into the field, regardless of season and weather, were necessary to a speedy termination of the war. . . . The armies in the East and West acted independently and without concert, like a balky team, no two ever pulling together."[2]

Grant went on to say that the armies had to press continuously, to give the Confederates no rest and to keep them from being able to move troops to threatened fronts. This is what Grant did, and how he won the American Civil War.

A quick summary of the plot of this book is compare and contrast, in that immortal high school phrase, the May 1863 Battle of Chancellorsville with the May 1864 Battle of the Wilderness. Virtually same location, similar tactical results, similar strategic realities, but as Grant realized when he took over, drastically different long-term results. What this book tries to answer, using the narrative, storytelling format and putting things in a larger context, is how and why such different results ensued.

The foundation of this book is the basic story it tells. The two core battles, Chancellorsville and the Wilderness, were major battles, fought under difficult conditions, with a fascinating and legendary cast of such leading men as Lee, Jackson, Hooker, Sickles, Howard, Stuart, Meade, and Grant. George McClellan is the eight-hundred-pound gorilla in the front of the story—though not a particularly active gorilla. William Sherman, the great hero/devil, is the very active twelve-hundred-pound gorilla lurking offstage at the back of the story. Abraham Lincoln stands over all the events narrated, as he searches for the answer of how to win the American Civil War and save the Union.

This story tells of the period when Lincoln found his answer, and found the men, in Grant and Sherman and some major supporting players such as George Thomas and Philip Sheridan, who could bring the answer to fruition. The focus is on the Eastern Theater of the Civil War, because this is the period in which the tide turned in this key theater.

One reason this story is important is that the Eastern theater of the Civil War was so important. The great debate continues among historians as to where the Civil War was won, in the East under Grant or in the West under Sherman. Looking at the military reality of the war, one would have to say that the West was more important. Northern successes in this theater enabled the North to damage and then destroy the Southern ability to supply its armies, including Lee's army in front of Richmond.

However, war is always political as well as military. Military realities are surprisingly irrelevant to this debate, as they were, if not irrelevant, then not the sole concern while the war was on. The East was the high-profile area of the war. The North could have won in the West, but if it lost in the East it might have lost the war. Ex post facto justification for policy is always risky. However, when the South did lose in the East, when Lee surrendered at Appomattox, it lost the war within a few weeks. This book, therefore, is the story of the period when the tide shifted in the key theater of the war.

The central event in this story, Grant's actions after the Battle of the Wilderness, is a tipping point, a historical contingency, a decision point where history can go one way or the other. Tipping points can be big and dramatic moments. These can be small moments, passing unnoticed at the time. Tipping points, decisive moments, frequently pick undramatic locations, such as the point on which this story turns. Decisive moments usually fail to announce that "this is a decisive moment," since by their very nature their decisiveness is likely to remain unknown for a long period of time. Decisive moments may not even be moments, and likely depend on appropriate and persistent follow-up to achieve lasting decisiveness. Tipping points occur. History comes to a point where things can go one way or the other. Things can also tip back.

Grant changed the literal and symbolic direction of the Civil War by recognizing and acting on something his predecessors had failed to recognize, or at least failed to carry out. Lee had learned the lesson during the Peninsula campaign, when by a series of battles, most of which he lost, he drove McClellan's Federal army away from Richmond. Battles have a context, and it is this context, the campaign, that most matters. The Battle of the Wilderness was, at best, a draw. But Grant realized that he had to look at more than the results of this battle, more than the stalemate amid this hellish forest. He had to keep going south, had to keep Lee and his weakened but still highly skilled and highly dangerous army, pinned in place until Grant could, if not defeat him in one stroke, pin him down and wear him out. The irony is that Grant did both. He pinned Lee at Petersburg, wore him down so Lee could no longer hold Petersburg and Richmond, and then chased him to Appomattox for the one stroke of cornering Lee and forcing his surrender.

Grant recognized that his context included coordination of other, simultaneous Federal efforts. Primary was William Sherman's effort in the West—to destroy the second main Confederate army and to rip the guts out of the Confederate economy and morale. Events elsewhere would affect events in Northern Virginia, and vice versa.

This story is one of appreciating context, of the need to act based on accurate information, of properly coordinating all available resources, of the need for flexibility (if Plan A does not work, try Plan B), of the need to choose a realistic and proper goal, of keeping the goal in sight, and doing what you need to do to reach the goal.

This book is the tool for telling its story. The story is valuable in the lessons it presents for today, as well as what it says about the past. Primarily, though, the story is exciting.

NOTES

EPIGRAPH

1. Theodore Irving, *"More Than Conqueror," or Memorials of Colonel J. Howard Kitching* (New York: Hurd and Houghton, 1873), 124.

INTRODUCTION

1. Eric Durschmied, *The Hinge Factor* (New York: Arcade Publishing, 1999), xvii.

CHAPTER ONE

1. O.R., Series I, Volume LI/1, 370, Scott to George McClellan, May 3, 1861.

2. Term is quoted on page 193, Daniel E. Sutherland, *Fredericksburg & Chancellorsville: The Dare Mark Campaign* (Lincoln and London: University of Nebraska Press, 1998).

3. Peter G. Tsouras, ed., *The Greenhill Dictionary of Military Quotations* (London: Greenhill Books; Mechanicsburg, PA: Stackpole Books, 2000), 366.

4. Bell I. Wiley, *Road to Appomattox* (Memphis: Memphis State College Press, 1956), 7.

5. United States Department of Homeland Security, Office of Immigration Statistics, "Table 1: Immigration to the United States; Fiscal Years 1820–2004," *2004 Yearbook of Immigration Statistics,* January 2006, 5.

6. Quoted in A. M. Williams, *Sam Houston and the War of Independence in Texas* (Boston: Houghton Mifflin Co., 1893), 353.

7. For a useful discussion of East versus West, see Historical Text Archive © 2003, http://www.historicaltextarchive.com/sections.php?op=viewarticle&artid=660. "The Confederate Military Effort in the West," by Craig L. Symonds.

8. Gary Kross, "Gettysburg Vignettes: Attack from the West, Vignette 1, Action on June 26," *Blue and Gray Magazine* (June 2000): 7–10, quote on page 7.

9. United States War Department, *The War of the Rebellion: A Compilation of the Official Records of the Union and Confederate Armies,* [OR], Washington, DC: GPO, 1880–1901; O.R., Series I, Volume LI/1, 370, Scott to McClellan, May 3, 1861.

10. Russell F. Weigley, *A Great Civil War* (Bloomington and Indianapolis: Indiana University Press, 2002), xxii, xxiii.

11. Edward Bates, *The Diary of Edward Bates, 1859–1866,* ed. Howard K. Beale (Washington, US Government Printing Office, 1933), 194.

12. Excerpt of speech of Captain William K. Martin on the mustering of his company (Henderson Guards, later Company K, 4th Texas Infantry Regiment), May 1861, Fincastle, Texas. Quoted in J. J. Faulk, *History of Henderson County, Texas* (Athens, TX: Athens Review Publishing Company, 1929), 129.

CHAPTER 2

1. Stephen D. Sears, ed., *The Civil War Papers of George B. McClellan: Selected Correspondence, 1861–1865* (New York: Ticknor & Fields, 1989), 211.

2. L. Thomas, Adjutant-General, to George McClellan, July 22, 1861, Series I, Volume II, 753.

3. Stephen W. Sears, *George B. McClellan: The Young Napoleon* (New York: Ticknor & Fields, 1988), 96.

4. Bruce Catton, *Mr. Lincoln's Army,* The Army of the Potomac, Volume I (Garden City, NY: Doubleday and Company, 1951, 1962), 61.

5. Doris Kearns Goodwin, *Team of Rivals: The Political Genius of Abraham Lincoln* (New York: Simon & Schuster, 2005), 383.

6. Sears, *George B. McClellan,* 113, 1861.

7. John Hay, *Inside Lincoln's White House: The Complete Civil War Diary of John Hay,* ed. Michael Burlingame and John R. Turner Ettlinger (Carbondale: Southern Illinois University Press, 1997), 32, entry for November 12, 1861.

8. Thomas J. Rowland, *George B. McClellan and Civil War History: In the Shadow of Grant and Sherman* (Kent, OH: Kent State University Press, 1998), 166–67.

9. Gary W. Gallagher, "A Civil War Watershed," in *The Richmond Campaign of 1862: The Peninsula and the Seven Days* (Chapel Hill: University of North Carolina Press, 2000), 3–27, quotation on page 5.

10. Josiah Gorgas, *The Journals of Josiah Gorgas, 1857–1878*, ed. Sarah Woolfolk Wiggins (Tuscaloosa: University of Alabama Press, 1995), 42–43.

11. Jeffry D. Wert, *The Sword of Lincoln* (New York: Simon & Schuster, 2005), 63.

12. Quoted in Wert, *The Sword of Lincoln*, 63.

13. Quoted in Stephen Sears, *To the Gates of Richmond: The Peninsula Campaign* (New York: Ticknor and Fields, 1992), 17.

14. Sears, *To the Gates of Richmond*, 17.

15. Reuven Bar-Levav, MD, *Thinking in the Shadow of Feelings* (New York: Simon and Schuster, 1988), 24.

16. Quoted in Sears, *Civil War Papers*, 128.

17. Joel H. Silbey, *A Respectable Minority: The Democratic Party in the Civil War Era, 1860–1868* (New York: Norton, 1977), ix.

18. The rank of admiral did not yet exist in the US Navy. "Flag Officer" and "Commodore" were honorary titles used for officers serving above the rank of captain.

19. McClellan to Goldsborough, April 5, 1862, 167, 229, in Sears, *George B. McClellan*, McClellan papers.

20. John G. Barnard, *The Peninsula Campaign and Its Antecedents* (New York: Van Nostrand, 1864), 74.

21. Quoted in Wert, *The Sword of Lincoln*, 69.

22. Wert, *The Sword of Lincoln*, 69.

23. O.R., Volume 11, Part I, 15.

24. James I. Robertson Jr., *Stonewall Jackson* (New York: MacMillan Publishing, 1997), 325.

25. Quoted in Robertson, *Stonewall Jackson*, 325.

26. Quoted in Robertson, *Stonewall Jackson*, 325.

27. John B. Jones, *A Rebel War Clark's Diary*, condensed, edited, and annotated by Earl Scheck Mires (New York: Sagamore Press, Inc., 1957), entry for March 2, 1861, 69.

28. Jones, *A Rebel War Clark's Diary*, May 8, 1862, 75.

29. Jones, *A Rebel War Clark's Diary*, May 14, 1862, 76.

30. Gustavus W. Smith, *Confederate War Papers* (New York: Atlantic Publishing, 1884), 181–82.

31. Edward A. Pollard, *Southern History of the War: The First Year of the War* (New York: Charles B. Richardson, 1864), 168.

32. Quoted in Sears, *To the Gates of Richmond*, 57.

33. Sears, *To the Gates of Richmond*, 57.

34. Cited in Russell F. Weigley, *A Great Civil War* (Bloomington: Indiana University Press, 2000), 132.

35. Philip Kearny, *Letters from the Peninsula: The Civil War Letters of General Philip Kearny*, ed. William B. Styple (Kearny, NJ: Belle Grove Publishing, 1988), 116.

36. Kearny, *Letters from the Peninsula*, 125.

37. Frederick Law Olmsted, *The Papers of Frederick Law Olmsted*, vol. 4, *Defending the Union: The Civil War and the U.S. Sanitary Commission*, ed. Jane Turner Censer (Baltimore: Johns Hopkins University Press, 1986), 389.

38. Olmsted, *The Papers of Frederick Law Olmsted*, 392–93.

CHAPTER 3

1. General Alpheus S. Williams, *From the Cannon's Mouth: The Civil War Letters of General Alpheus S. Williams*, edited with an introduction by Milo M. Quaife (Detroit: Wayne State University Press, 1959), 125.

2. Russell Weigley, *A Great Civil War* (Bloomington and Indianapolis: Indiana University Press, 2000), 136.

3. O.R., Series I, Volume 12, part 3, 473–74.

4. Edward J. Stackpole, *From Cedar Mountain to Antietam* (Harrisburg, PA: The Stackpole Company, 1993), 23.

5. Major General John Pope, General Orders No. 5, July 18, 1862, text found in John Codman Ropes, *The Army under Pope* (New York: C. Scribner's Sons, 1885), 174.

6. Pope, General Orders No. 7, July 18, 1862, text found in Ropes, 175.

7. Major General John Pope, General Orders No. 11, July 23, 1862, text found in Ropes 176–77.

8. Stackpole, *From Cedar Mountain to Antietam*, 24.

9. Major General John Pope, General Orders No. 19, August 14, 1862, text found at http://www.civilwarhome.com/popesorders.htm.

10. Robert E. Lee, *The Wartime Papers of R. E. Lee* (Boston: Little, Brown, 1961), 519.

11. O.R. Volume XIX, Part 2, 590. Robert E. Lee to Jefferson Davis, September 3, 1862.

12. Herman Hattaway and Archer Jones, *How the North Won: A Military History of the Civil War* (Urbana: University of Illinois Press, 1983), quoted page 234.

13. Joseph L. Harsh, *Taken at the Flood: Robert E. Lee and Confederate Strategy in the Maryland Campaign* of 1862 (Kent, OH: Kent State University Press, 1999), 57.

14. William Allan, *The Army of Northern Virginia in 1862* (Dayton, OH: Morningside House, 1984), 200.

15. Bruce Catton, *The Army of the Potomac: Mr. Lincoln's Army* (Garden City, NY: Doubleday & Company, Inc., 1951 and 1962), 220–21.

16. Henry Kyd Douglas, *I Rode with Stonewall* (New York: Ballantine Books, 1974), 152.

17. Stephen D. Sears, ed., *The Civil War Papers of George B. McClellan: Selected Correspondence, 1861–1865* (New York: Ticknor & Fields, 1989), 280.

18. Sears, *George B. McClellan*, 282.

19. Pages 430–32 in James Thomas Flexner, *George Washington in the American Revolution (1775–1783)* (Boston and Toronto: Little, Brown and Company, 1967), provide details on some of the measures Washington took in late summer 1781 to convince the British he was planning to attack New York City when he was actually planning a move south to Yorktown, Virginia.

20. Gary Gallagher, "The Generalship of Robert E. Lee," *North & South*, Volume 3, no. 5 (June 2000): 10–18, quotation from page 15.

21. Catton, *Mr. Lincoln's Army*, 252.

22. Jeffry D. Wert, *The Sword of Lincoln* (New York: Simon & Schuster, 2005), quoted 155.

23. Quoted in Wert, *The Sword of Lincoln*, 155.

24. O.R., McClellan Report, October 15, 1862, 30.

25. Wert, *The Sword of Lincoln*, 157.

26. A. Williams, *From the Cannon's Mouth*, 125.

27. James M. McPherson, *Crossroads of Freedom* (New York: Oxford University Press, 2001), 3.

28. See William A. Frassanito, *Antietam: The Photographic Legacy of America's Bloodiest Day* (New York: Charles Scribner's Sons, 1978), 197–223.

29. Robert K. Krick, "It Appeared as Though Mutual Extermination Would Put a Stop to the Awful Carnage," in Gary W. Gallagher, ed., *The Antietam Campaign* (Chapel Hill and London: University of North Carolina Press, 1999), 222–58, quote on page 223.

30. George N. Smalley, New York "Tribune" Narrative, September 17, 1862, reprinted in Frank Moore, ed., *Rebellion Record, Volume V* (New York: Arno Press reprint, 1977), 466–72, quote on page 472.

31. Smalley, New York "Tribune" Narrative, 472.

32. Smalley, New York "Tribune" Narrative, 472.

33. Ronald H. Bailey and the editors of Time-Life Books, *The Battle of Antietam* (Alexandria, VA: Time-Life Books, 1984), quoted on page 139.

34. Frank L. Byrne and Andrew T. Weaver, eds., *Haskell of Gettysburg: His Life and Civil War Papers* (1970; Kent, OH: Kent State University Press, 1989), 48.

35. William H. Powell, *The Fifth Army Corps* (1895; Dayton, OH: Morningside, 1984), 302.

36. Alexander Webb to his father, September 24, 1862, Webb Papers, Yale University Library, quoted in Sears, *McClellan*, 320.

37. George G. Meade, *The Life and Letters of General George Gordon Meade, Volume I*, two volumes (New York: Scribner's, 1913), 311.

38. Josiah Marshall Favill, *The Diary of a Young Officer* (Chicago: Donnelley, 1909), 191.

39. Abraham Lincoln, *The Literary Works of Abraham Lincoln*, selected, with an introduction, by Carl Van Doren (New York: The Heritage Press, 1942), 222.

40. Catton, *Mr. Lincoln's Army*, 328.

41. Herman Haupt, *Reminiscences of General Herman Haupt* (Milwaukee: Wright and Joss, 1901), 160.

42. Peter W. Alexander, Savannah Republican, reprinted in *Macon Journal & Messenger*, October 8, 1862.

43. Gary W. Gallagher, "The Net Result of the Campaign Was in Our Favor: Confederate Reaction to the Maryland Campaign," 3–43 in Gary W. Gallagher, ed., *The Antietam Campaign* (Chapel Hill and London: University of North Carolina Press, 1999), quote on page 34.

CHAPTER 4

1. Quoted on page 80, Stephen W. Sears, *Chancellorsville* (Boston and New York: Houghton Mifflin Company, 1996).

2. William Marvel, "The Making of a Myth: Ambrose E. Burnside and the Union High Command at Fredericksburg," in *The Fredericksburg Campaign*, ed. Gary W. Gallagher (Chapel Hill and London: University of North Carolina Press, 1995), 1–25.

3. Marvel, "The Making of a Myth," 2.

4. Bruce Catton, *Army of the Potomac: Glory Road* (New York: Doubleday, 1952), 19.

5. John Edmund Gough, *Fredericksburg and Chancellorsville: A Study of the Federal Operations* (London: H. Ress, Ltd., 1913), 53.

6. *The Literary Works of Abraham Lincoln, Volume VI*, selected, with an introduction, by Carl van Doren (New York: The Heritage Press, 1942), December 22, 1862, "Congratulations to the Army of the Potomac," 13.

7. William Stoddard, *Inside the White House in War Times* (New York: C. L. Webster and Co., 1880), 101.

8. Geoffrey Perret, *Lincoln's War* (New York: Random House, 2004), 347.

9. Sears, *Chancellorsville*, 81.

10. United States Government, War Department, *The War of the Rebellion: A Compilation of the Official Records of the Union and Confederate Armies*, Washington, D.C.: Government Printing Office, 1880–1901, Series I, Volume XXV, Part 2, Union Correspondence Etc. #1. Found Guild Press of Indiana, Inc., The Civil War CD-ROM, v 1.6. *The Literary Works of Abraham Lincoln*, selected, with an introduction, by Carl Van Doren (New York: The Heritage Press, 1942), 231.

11. Numa Barned to sister, March 27, 1863, Numa Barned Papers, William L. Clements Library, University of Michigan. Quote by John Hennessy, 27, "We Shall Make Richmond Howl: The Army of the Potomac on the Eve of Chancellorsville,"

1–35, in Gary W. Gallagher, ed., *Chancellorsville: The Battle and Its Aftermath* (Chapel Hill and London: University of North Carolina Press, 1996).

12. Hennessy, "We Shall Make Richmond Howl," 13.

13. George Breck, letter, *Rochester Union and Advertiser*, April 17, 1863.

14. Sears, *Chancellorsville*, 74–75.

CHAPTER 5

1. Edward Porter Alexander, *Fighting for the Confederacy*, ed. Gary W. Gallagher (Chapel Hill and London: University of North Carolina Press, 1989), 195.

2. Noah Brooks, *Mr. Lincoln's Washington: Selections from the Writings of Noah Brooks, Civil War Correspondent*, ed. P. J. Staudenraus (South Brunswick, NJ: T. Yoseloff, 1967), 148.

3. Brooks, *Mr. Lincoln's Washington*, 150.

4. Darius N. Couch, "The Chancellorsville Campaign," in *Battles and Leaders of the Civil War, Volume III*, eds. Robert Underwood Johnson and Clarence Clough Buel (Edison, NJ: Castle Books, 1995 reprint), 154–72, quote on page 155.

5. Quoted Stephen W. Sears, *Chancellorsville* (Boston and New York: Houghton Mifflin Company, 1996), 116–17.

6. Sears, *Chancellorsville*, quote on page 120.

7. Edward G. Longacre, *The Commanders of Chancellorsville* (Nashville: Rutledge Hill Press, 2005), 80.

8. Alexander K. McClure, *Colonel Alexander K. McClure's Recollections of Half a Century* (New York: AMS Press reprint, 1976), 348.

9. McClure, *Colonel Alexander K. McClure's Recollections*, 348.

10. Sears, *Chancellorsville*, quote on page 120.

11. Alexander, *Fighting for the Confederacy*, 195.

12. Quoted in Sears, *Chancellorsville*, 140.

13. Sears, *Chancellorsville*, 101.

14. Quoted in Sears, *Chancellorsville*, 101.

15. T. S. C. Lowe to Major General D. Butterfield, Chief of Staff, Army of the Potomac, April 12, 1863, quoted in Eugene B. Block, *Above the Civil War* (Berkeley, CA: Howell-North Books, 1966), 171.

16. *Charleston Mercury*, December 15, 1862.

17. Butterfield to Sedgwick, April 29, 1863, United States War Department, *The War of the Rebellion: A Compilation of the Official Records of the Union and Confederate Armies*, Washington, DC: Government Printing Office, 1880–1901, Series I, Volume XXV, part 2, 292.

18. Williams to Sedgwick, April 30, 1863, O.R. Series I, Volume XXV, part 2, 306.

19. Chancellorsville Address of General Fitzhugh Lee before the Virginia Division, A.N.V. Association, October 29th, 1879, Southern Historical Society Papers, Vol. VII. Richmond, Va., December, 1879. No. 12, 562.

20. O.R., Volume 25, part 2, 756, 757.

21. Charles Marshall, "Events Leading Up to the Battle of Gettysburg," *Southern Historical Society Papers*, Volume 23 (1895): 205–9, quotation on page 210.

22. April 30, 1863, Official Records, 23:1, 171.

23. Quoted in Theodore Irving, *"More Than Conqueror," or Memorials of Colonel J. Howard Kitching* (New York: Hurd and Houghton, 1873), 124.

24. Rice C. Bull, *Soldiering: The Civil War Diary of Rice C. Bull, 123rd New York Volunteer Infantry*, ed. K. Jack Bauer (San Rafael, CA: Presidio Press, 1977), 44–45.

25. John Bigelow Jr., *The Campaign of Chancellorsville* (New Haven: Yale University Press, 1910), 154.

26. James Power Smith, *Stonewall Jackson and Chancellorsville*, Richmond: R. E. Lee Camp No 1, Confederate Veterans, 1904, 15.

27. Smith, *Stonewall Jackson*, 14.

28. Quoted in James I. Robertson Jr., *Stonewall Jackson: The Man, The Soldier, The Legend* (New York: Macmillan USA, 1997), xiii.

29. Chancellorsville, https://civilwarhome.com/fleechancellorsville.html.

30. Quoted in Robertson, *Stonewall Jackson*, 721.

31. Couch, *Battles and Leaders*, 163.

32. Augustus C. Hamlin, *The Battle of Chancellorsville; the Attack of Stonewall Jackson and His Army upon the Right Flank of the Army of the Potomac at Chancellorsville, Virginia, on Saturday Afternoon, May 2, 1863* (Bangor, ME: author, 1986), 125.

33. Hamlin, *The Battle of Chancellorsville*, 128.

34. Couch, *Battles and Leaders*, 164.

35. Couch, *Battles and Leaders*, 170.

36. Samuel P. Bates, "Hooker's Comments on Chancellorsville," *Battles and Leaders, Volume II*, 215–23, quote on page 222.

37. Couch, *Battles and Leaders*, 171.

38. Jedediah Hotchkiss, *Make Me a Map of the Valley: The Civil War Journal of Stonewall Jackson's Topographer*, ed. Archie P. McDonald, foreword by T. Harry Williams (Dallas: Southern Methodist University Press, 1973), 143, entry for May 12, 1863.

39. General Edward Porter Alexander, *Fighting for the Confederacy: The Personal Recollections of General Edward Porter Alexander*, ed. Gary W. Gallagher (Chapel Hill and London: University of North Carolina Press, 1989), 217.

40. Weigley, xxiv.

41. Lee, quoted by John Sedden, 1863, in *Southern Historical Society Papers* 4 (1877): 153–54.

42. Edward G. Longacre, *The Commanders of Chancellorsville* (Nashville: Rutledge Hill Press, 2005), in particular page 280.

43. Longacre, *The Commanders of Chancellorsville*, 280.

44. Couch, *Battles and Leaders*, 171.

45. Sears, *Chancellorsville*, 504–5.

CHAPTER 6

1. Abraham Lincoln, *The Literary Works of Abraham Lincoln*, selected, with an introduction, by Carl Van Doren (New York: The Heritage Press, 1942), 292.

2. Carl Sandburg, *Abraham Lincoln: The War Years, Volume II* (New York: Harcourt, Brace & Company, 1939), 97.

3. Charles H. Banes, *History of the Philadelphia Brigade* (Philadelphia: J. B. Lippincott & Co., 1876), 164–65.

4. O.R., Volume 25, part 2, 438.

5. O.R., Volume 25, part 2, 449.

6. Geoffrey Perret, *Lincoln's War* (New York: Random House, 2004), 247.

7. O.R., Volume 25, part 2, 438.

8. Quoted Noah Andre Trudeau, *Gettysburg: A Testing of Courage* (New York: Perennial, 2002), 11.

9. Quoted in Trudeau, *Gettysburg*, 12.

10. Quoted in Trudeau, *Gettysburg*, 14.

11. Stephen Minot Weld, *War Diary and Papers of Stephen Minot Weld* (Cambridge, MA: Riverside Press, 1912), 210.

12. Walter H. Taylor, *Four Years with General Lee*, ed. James Robertson (New York: Bonanza Books, 1962), 93.

13. Henry Hatch, "Letter to J. William Jones," *Southern Historical Society Papers* 4, No. 4 (October 1877): 151–60, quoted on page 157.

14. *The War of the Rebellion*, Volume XXVII, Part 2, 317–19.

15. Quoted in Edwin B. Coddington, *The Gettysburg Campaign: A Study in Command* (New York: Charles Scribner's Sons, 1968), 361.

16. James Longstreet, "The Campaign of Gettysburg," *Philadelphia Weekly Times*, November 3, 1877.

17. Warren to Farley, July 13, 1872, Quoted in Henry J. Hunt, "The Second Day at Gettysburg," *Battles and Leaders of the Civil War, Volume 3*, eds. Robert U. Johnson and Clarence C. Buell (New York: Century Company, 1884–1889), 307.

18. Oliver W. Norton, *Strong Vincent and His Brigade at Gettysburg* (Chicago: [No Publisher Listed], 1909). Found in manuscript room, Library of Congress, Washington, DC., 6–7.

19. *The War of the Rebellion: A Compilation of the Official Records of the Union and Confederate Armies*, Washington, DC: Government Printing Office, 1889. Series I, Volume XXVII, Part I, 623.

20. O.R., Vol XXVII, Part I, 623.

21. William C. Oates, "Account of Col. William C. Oates, 15th Alabama" type-script found at Gettysburg National Park Service library, LRT 15th Alabama, noted on document "Manuscript in Bowdoin College Library."

22. Oates, "Account of Col. William C. Oates," 212.

23. Oates, "Account of Col. William C. Oates."

24. O.R., Series I, Volume XXVII, Part I, 623.

25. Chamberlain to General Barnes, commanding division, September 3rd, 1863. From the collections of the New York Historical Society.

26. Chamberlain to Governor Abner Coburn, Governor of Maine, July 21, 1863, Joshua L. Chamberlain papers, Library of Congress.

27. O.R., Series I, Volume XXVII, 624.

28. Oates, "Account of Col. William C. Oates."

29. George R. Stewart, *Pickett's Charge* (Boston: Houghton Mifflin Company, 1959), 113.

30. Ernest B. Furgurson, *Chancellorsville 1863: The Souls of the Brave* (New York: Alfred A. Knopf, 1993), 350.

31. Robert Underwood Johnson and Clarence Clough Buel, eds., *Battles and Leaders of the Civil War, Volume III* (Edison, NJ: Castle Books, 1995 reprint), 246.

32. Trudeau, 526.

33. Doris Kearns Goodwin, *Team of Rivals: The Political Genius of Abraham Lincoln* (New York: Simon & Schuster, 2005), 535.

34. John S. Mosby, *The Memoirs of Colonel John S. Mosby*, ed. Charles Welles Russell (1917; Bloomington: Indiana University Press, 1959), 381.

CHAPTER 7

1. Abraham Lincoln, *The Literary Works of Abraham Lincoln*, selected, with an introduction, by Carl Van Doren (New York: The Heritage Press, 1942), 242.

2. Douglas Putnam Jr., "Reminiscences of the Battle of Shiloh," *Sketches of War History, 1861–1865*, Military Order of the Loyal Legal of the United States, Ohio Commandary, Volume 3, 197–211.

3. James Harrison Wilson, *Under the Old Flag; Recollections of Military Operations in the War for the Union, the Spanish War, the Boxer Rebellion, etc.* (Westwood, CT: Greenwood Press, 1971), 17.

4. Wilson, *Under the Old Flag*, 17.

5. Ulysses S. Grant, *Personal Memoirs of U.S. Grant* (New York: The Library of America, 1990), 246.

6. Charles E. Wilcox, "With Grant at Vicksburg," 467, Edgar L. Erickson, ed., *Journal of the Illinois State Historical Society*, Volume XXX, No. 4 (January 1938).

7. Mary A. Loughborough, *My Cave Life in Vicksburg* (CreateSpace Independent Publishing Platform), 56–58.

8. Lincoln, *The Literary Works of Abraham Lincoln*, 242.

9. Lincoln, *The Literary Works of Abraham Lincoln*, 242.

10. Edwin B. Coddington, *The Gettysburg Campaign: A Study in Command* (New York: Charles Scribner's Sons, 1868), 572.

11. Lincoln, *The Literary Works of Abraham Lincoln*, 243–44.

12. George Gordon Meade (General Meade's son), ed., *Life and Letters of George Gordon Meade, Major General, United States Army, Volume II* (New York: Charles Scribner's Sons, 1913), 191.

13. Bruce Catton, *A Stillness at Appomattox,* The Army of the Potomac, Volume III (Garden City, NY: Doubleday and Company, Inc., 1953), 43.

14. Horace Porter, *Campaigning with Grant* (New York: The Century Company, 1897), 46–47.

15. Albert D. Richardson, *A Personal History of Ulysses S. Grant* (Hartford, CT: American Publishing Company, 1868), 194.

16. Donald C. Pfanz, *Richard S. Ewell: A Soldier's Life* (Chapel Hill and London: University of North Carolina Press, 1998), 589.

17. July 22, 1865, Report of Lieutenant General Ulysses S. Grant, U.S. Army, Commanding Armies of the United States, including operations March, 1864–May, 1865, O.R., Series I, Volume XXXVI, Part I, 12–13.

18. Brooks D. Simpson, "Great Expectations," 1–35, in Gary W. Gallagher, ed., *The Wilderness Campaign* (Chapel Hill and London: University of North Carolina Press, 1997).

19. Andrew A. Humphreys, *The Virginia Campaign of '64 and '65* (New York and London: Thomas Yoseloff, 1963 reprint), 5, 6.

20. Grant, *Personal Memoirs of U.S. Grant*, 486.

21. Official Records, Series I, Volume XXXIII, 1144.

22. J. William Jones, *Life and Letters of Robert E. Lee, Soldier and Man* (Washington, DC: The Neale Publishing Company, 1906), 50.

23. O.R. Series I, Volume XXXIII, 828, Grant to Meade, April 9, 1864.

24. Humphreys, *The Virginia Campaign of '64 and '65*, 9.

25. Humphreys, *The Virginia Campaign of '64 and '65*, 9–10.

26. Humphreys, *The Virginia Campaign of '64 and '65*, 10–11.

27. Humphreys, *The Virginia Campaign of '64 and '65*, 11.

28. Frank Wilkeson, *Recollections of a Private Soldier in the Army of the Potomac* (New York: G. P. Putnam's Sons, 1887), 39–41.

CHAPTER 8

1. Horace Porter, *Campaigning with Grant* (New York: The Century Company, 1897), 46–47.

2. Alexander S. Webb, "Through the Wilderness," in *Battles and Leaders of the Civil War: The Way to Appomattox, Volume IV*, eds. Robert Underwood Johnston and Clarence Buel (New York: Castle Books Reprint 1956), 152–69, 154.

3. Frank Wilkeson, *Recollections of a Private Soldier in the Army of the Potomac* (New York: G. P. Putnam's Sons, 1887), 49–54.

4. O.R., Volume 36, part 2, 403.

5. Ulysses S. Grant, *Personal Memoirs of U.S. Grant* (New York: The Library of America, 1990), 527.

6. Gordon C. Rhea, *The Battle of the Wilderness* (Baton Rouge: Louisiana State University Press, 1994), 104.

7. Variation on this point raised in an email to me from Greg Mertz, supervisory historian, Fredericksburg and Spotsylvania National Military Park, June 19, 2006.

8. Amos M. Judson, *History of the Eighty-Third Regiment Pennsylvania Volunteers* (Erie, PA: B. F. H. Lyon, 1865), 192.

9. Brevett-Major Holman S. Melcher, "An Experience in the Battle of the Wilderness," *War Papers Read before the Commandery of the State of Maine, Military Order of the Loyal Legion of the United States* (3 volumes), Portland, Maine: Military Order, 1898, Volume I, 73–84. Story is also told in John J. Pullen, *The Twentieth Maine* (1957; Dayton, OH: Morningside Bookshop, 1984), 177–94.

10. All direct quotes, unless noted, in this section are from Melcher, "An Experience in the Battle of the Wilderness," 76–82.

11. See discussion of the bayonet in Brent Nosworthy, *The Bloody Crucible of Courage* (New York: Carroll & Graf, 2003), 594–608.

12. Curtis S. King, William Glenn Robertson, and Steven E. Clay, *Staff Ride Handbook for the Overland Campaign, Virginia, 4 May to 15 June 1864: A Study in Operational-Level Command* (Fort Leavenworth, KS: Combat Studies Institute Press, 2006), 53.

13. Rhea, *The Battle of the Wilderness*, quoted on page 291.

14. King et al., *Staff Ride Handbook*, 54.

15. Quoted Harold B. Simpson, *Hood's Texas Brigade: Lee's Grenadier Guard* (Waco, TX: Texian Press, 1970), 396.

16. Quoted in Simpson, *Hood's Texas Brigade*, 397.

17. Simpson, *Hood's Texas Brigade*, 397–98.

18. James Longstreet, *From Manassas to Appomattox* (Bloomington, IN: Indiana University Press, 1960 reprint), 568.

19. Porter, *Campaigning with Grant*, 68–70.

20. King, Curtis S., William Glenn Robertson, and Steven E. Clay, *Staff Ride Handbook for the Overland Campaign, Virginia, 4 May to 15 June 1874: A Study in Operational-Level Command* (Fort Leavenworth, KS: Combat Studies Institute Press), 2006, 58.

21. Grant, *Personal Memoirs of U.S. Grant*, 210.

CHAPTER 9

1. For more detailed coverage of the Petersburg campaign, see my book, *Petersburg* (Philadelphia: Chelsea House Publishers, 2003).

2. July 22, 1865, Report of Lieutenant General Ulysses S. Grant, U.S. Army, Commanding Armies of the United States, including operations March, 1864–May, 1865, *Official Records of the War of the Rebellion*, Washington, DC: Government Printing Office, 1880–1900, Series I, Volume XXXVI, Part I, 12.

3. Noah Andre Trudeau, "The Walls of 1864," in *With My Face to the Enemy: Perspectives on the Civil War*, ed. Robert Cowley (New York: G. P. Putnam's Sons, 2001), 413–28.

4. John Hay, *Inside Lincoln's White House: The Complete Civil War Diary of John Hay*, eds. Michael Burlingame and John R. Turner Ettlinger (Carbondale: Southern Illinois University Press, 1997), 195.

5. Bruce Catton, *A Stillness at Appomattox: The Army of the Potomac Trilogy* (New York: Anchor Books, 2010), 186.

6. Quoted in Catton, *A Stillness at Appomattox: The Army of the Potomac Trilogy*, 191.

7. Frank Wilkeson, *Recollections of a Private Soldier in the Army of the Potomac* (New York: G. P. Putnam's Sons, 1887), 162.

8. G. T. Beauregard, "Four Days at Petersburg," in *The Way to Appomattox: Battles and Leaders of the Civil War, Volume IV*, eds. Robert Underwood Johnson and Clarence Clough Bell (New York: Castle Books, 1956), 540–44, reprint of original edition, 541.

9. Noah Andre Trudeau, *The Last Citadel: Petersburg, Virginia June 1864–April 1865* (Baton Rouge: Louisiana State University Press, 1993), 53.

10. Quoted in Doris Kearns Goodwin, *Team of Rivals: The Political Genius of Abraham Lincoln* (New York: Simon & Schuster, 2005), 648.

CHAPTER 10

1. The title has been "stolen" from the title of the last chapter of my Petersburg book cited.

2. Abraham Lincoln, *The Literary Works of Abraham Lincoln*, selected, with an introduction, by Carl Van Doren (New York: The Heritage Press, 1942), 276.

3. Horace Porter, *Campaigning with Grant* (New York: The Century Company, 1897), 432.

4. Bruce Catton, *A Stillness at Appomattox: The Army of the Potomac Trilogy* (New York: Anchor Books, 2010), 358.

5. John B. Jones, *A Rebel War Clark's Diary*, condensed, edited, and annotated by Earl Scheck Mires (New York: Sagamore Press, Inc., 1957), entry for April 2, 1865, 526.

6. Derek Smith, *Lee's Last Stand* (Shippensburg, PA: White Mane Books, 2002), 1.

7. Edward M. Boykin, Lieutenant Colonel, 7th South Carolina Cavalry, *The Falling Flag* (New York: E. J. Hale and Son, Publishers, 1874), 12–13.

CHAPTER 11

1. Colonel Thomas X. Hammes, USMC, ret., *The Sling and the Stone: On Warfare in the 21st Century* (St. Paul, MN: Zenith Press, MBI Publishing Company, 2004), 290.

2. July 22, 1865, Report of Lieutenant General Ulysses S. Grant, U.S. Army, Commanding Armies of the United States, including operations March, 1864–May, 1865, OR, Series I, Volume XXXVI, Part I, 12–13.

BIBLIOGRAPHY

1864: Grinding, Relentless War. Special magazine issue by Primedia, 1984.

Alexander, Edward Porter. *Fighting for the Confederacy.* Edited by Gary W. Gallagher. Chapel Hill: University of North Carolina Press, 1989.

Alexander, Peter W. *Savannah Republican*, reprinted in *Macon Journal & Messenger*, October 8, 1862.

Allan, William. *The Army of Northern Virginia in 1862.* Dayton, OH: Morningside House, 1984.

Ayers, Edward L. *What Caused the Civil War?* New York: W. W. Norton & Co., 2005.

Bailey, Ronald H., and the editors of Time-Life Books, *The Battle of Antietam.* Alexandria, VA: Time-Life Books, 1984.

Banes, Charles H. *History of the Philadelphia Brigade.* Philadelphia: J. B. Lippincott & Co, 1876.

Bates, Edward, *The Diary of Edward Bates, 1859-1866*, edited by Howard K. Beale, Washington, DC: U.S. Government Printing Office, 1933

Bar Levav, Reuven, M.D., *Thinking in the Shadow of Feelings.* New York: Simon & Schuster, 1988.

Barnard, John G. *The Peninsula Campaign and Its Antecedents.* New York: Van Nostrand, 1864.

Bates, Edward. *The Diary of Edward Bates, 1859-1866*, edited by Howard K. Beale. Washington, DC: U.S. Government Printing Office, 1933.

Bates, Samuel P. "Hooker's Comments on Chancellorsville," *Battles and Leaders of the Civil War,* edited by Robert U. Johnson and Clarence C. Buel. New York: Century Company, 1884–1889. Vol. 3, 215–23.

Beauregard, G. T. "Four Days at Petersburg," edited by Robert Underwood Johnson and Clarence Clough Buel, *The Way to Appomattox: Battles and Leaders of the Civil War*. New York: Castle Books, Vol. 4, 540–44; 1956 reprint of original edition.

Bigelow, John , Jr. *The Campaign of Chancellorsville*. New Haven, CT: Yale University Press, 1910.

Block, Eugene B. *Above the Civil War*. Berkeley, CA: Howell-North Books, 1966.

Boykin, Edward M., Lieutenant Colonel, 7th South Carolina Cavalry, *The Falling Flag*. New York: E. J. Hale and Son, Publishers, 1874.

Brager, Bruce L. *Petersburg*. Philadelphia: Chelsea House, Publishers, 2003.

Brands, H. W. *Lone Star Nation*. New York: Doubleday, 2004.

Breck, George, letter. *Rochester Union and Advertiser*, April 17, 1863.

Brooks, Noah. *Mr. Lincoln's Washington: Selections from the Writings of Noah Brooks, Civil War Correspondent*, edited by P. J. Staudenraus. South Brunswick, NJ: T. Yoseloff, 1967.

Bull, Rice C. *Soldiering: The Civil War Diary of Rice C. Bull, 123rd New York Volunteer Infantry*, edited by K. Jack Bauer. San Rafael, CA: Presidio Press, 1977.

Byrne, Frank L. and Andrew T. Weaver, editors. *Haskell of Gettysburg: His Life and Civil War Papers*. Kent, OH: Kent State University Press, 1989 reprint of 1970 book.

Catton, Bruce. *A Stillness at Appomattox*. Garden City, NY: Doubleday and Company, Inc., 1953.

Catton, Bruce. *Mr. Lincoln's Army*. Garden City, NY: Doubleday and Company, 1951, 1962.

Catton, Bruce. *Glory Road*. Garden City, NY: Doubleday and Company, 1952.

Chamberlain, Joshua Lawrence to General Barnes, commanding division, September 3, 1863. From the collections of the New York Historical Society.

Chamberlain, Joshua Lawrence to Governor Abner Coburn, Governor of Maine, July 21, 1863. Joshua L. Chamberlain papers, Library of Congress.

Charleston Mercury, December 15, 1862.

Coddington, Edwin B. *The Gettysburg Campaign: A Study in Command*. New York: Charles Scribner's Sons, 1968.

Couch, Darius N. "The Chancellorsville Campaign," in Robert Underwood Johnson and Clarence Clough Buel, editors, *Battles and Leaders of the Civil War*, Vol. 3. Edison, NJ: Castle Books, 1995 reprint.

Doubleday, Abner. *Chancellorsville and Gettysburg*. New York: C. Scribner's Sons, 1882.

Douglas, Henry Kyd. *I Rode With Stonewall*. New York: Ballantine Books, 1974.

Dowdy, Clifford, *Lee and his Men at Gettysburg: The Death of a Nation*. Lincoln: University of Nebraska Press, 1999, (reprint) 1958.

Durschmied, Erik. *The Hinge Factor*. New York: Arcade Publishing, 1999.

Faulk, J. J. *History of Henderson County, Texas*. Athens, TX: Athens Review Publishing Company, 1929.

Favill, Joshua Marshall. *The Diary of a Young Officer*. Chicago: Donnelley, 1909.

Fehrenbacher, Don E. *The Slaveholding Republic*. Completed and edited by Warm M. McAfee. New York: Oxford University Press, 2001.

Fordney, Ben Fuller. *Stoneman at Chancellorsville: The Coming of Age of Union Cavalry*. Shippensburg, PA: White Mane Books, 1998.

Frassanito, William A. *Antietam: The Photographic Legacy of America's Bloodiest Day*. New York: Charles Scribner's Sons, 1978.

Furgurson, Ernest B. *Chancellorsville 1863: The Souls of the Brave*. New York: Alfred A. Knopf, 1993.

Gallagher, Gary W. "The Generalship of Robert E. Lee." *North & South*. Vol. 3, Number 5, June 2000, 10–18.

Gallagher, Gary W. "A Civil War Watershed," in Gary W. Gallagher, editor, *The Richmond Campaign of 1862: The Peninsula and the Seven Days*. Chapel Hill: University of North Carolina Press, 2000, 3–27.

Gallagher, Gary W. "The Net Result of the Campaign was in Our Favor: Confederate Reaction to the Maryland Campaign," Gary W. Gallagher, editor, *The Antietam Campaign*, Chapel Hill: The University of North Carolina Press, 1999, 3–43.

Gallagher, Gary W. "The Generals Who Brought Dixie Down." *New York Times*, October 21, 1990, http://query.nytimes.com/gst/fullpage.html?res=9D0CEED8 153FF932A15753C1A966958260&sec=&pagewanted=print

Goodwin, Doris Kearns. *Team of Rivals: The Political Genius of Abraham Lincoln*. New York: Simon & Schuster, 2005.

Gorgas, Josiah. *The Journals of Josiah Gorgas, 1857–1878. Edited by* Sarah Woolfolk Wiggins, Tuscaloosa: University of Alabama Press, 1995.

Gough, John Edmund. *Fredericksburg and Chancellorsville: A Study of the Federal Operations*. London: H. Ress, Ltd., 1913.

Grant, Ulysses S. *Memoirs and Selected Letters*. New York: Library of America, 1990 [1 volume reprint]

Hamlin, Augustus C. *The Battle of Chancellorsville; the Attack of Stonewall Jackson and his Army upon the Right Flank of the Army of the Potomac at Chancellorsville, Virginia, on Saturday Afternoon, May 2, 1863*. Bangor, ME: The author, 1896.

Hammes, Colonel Thomas X, USMC, Ret. *The Sling and the Stone: On Warfare in the 21st Century*. St. Paul: MN: Zenith Press, MBI Publishing Company, 2004.

Harsh, Joseph L. *Taken at the Flood: Robert E. Lee and Confederate Strategy in the Maryland Campaign*. Kent, OH: Kent State University Press, 1999.

Hattaway, Herman and Archer Jones. *How the North Won: A Military History of the Civil War*. Urbana: University of Illinois Press, 1983.

Haupt, Herman. *Reminiscences of General Herman Haupt*. Milwaukee, WI: Wright and Joss, 1901.

Hay, John. *Inside Lincoln's White House: The Complete Civil War Diary of John Hay*. Edited by Michael Burlingname and John R. Turner Ettlinger. Carbondale: Southern Illinois University Press, 1997.

Hennessey, John. "We Shall Make Richmond Howl: The Army of the Potomac on the Eve of Chancellorsville," Gary W. Gallagher, editor, *Chancellorsville: The Battle and its Aftermath*. Chapel Hill: The University of North Carolina Press, 1996, 1–35.

Heth, Henry. "Letter to J. William Jones," *Southern Historical Society Papers*. Vol. 4, Number 4, October 1877, pages 151–60. Historical Text Archive © 2003. http://www.historicaltextarchive.com/sections.php?op=viewarticle&artid=660

Hotchkiss, Jedediah. *Make me a Map of the Valley: The Civil War Journal of Stonewall Jackson's Topographer*. Edited by Archie P. McDonald, foreword by T. Harry Williams, Dallas, TX: Southern Methodist University Press, 1973.

Humphreys, Andrew A. *The Virginia Campaign of '64 and '65*. New Yorkn: Thomas Yoseloff, 1963 reprint.

Hunt, Henry J. "The Second Day at Gettysburg," *Battles and Leaders of the Civil War*. Edited by Robert U. Johnson and Clarence C. Buel. New York: Century Company, 1884–1889. Vol. 3, 290–313.

Irving, Theodore. *More Than Conqueror: Memorials of J. Howard Kitching*. New York: Hurd and Houghton, 1873.

Jones, J. William. *Life and Letters of Robert E. Lee, Soldier and Man*, Washington, DC: The Neale Publishing Company, 1906.

Jones, John B. *A Rebel War Clark's Diary*. Condensed, edited, and annotated by Earl Schenck Miers. New York: Sagamore Press, Inc. 1957.

Judson, Amos M. *History of the Eighty-Third Regiment Pennsylvania Volunteers*. Erie, PA: B. F. H. Lyon, 1865.

Kearny, Philip. *Letters from the Peninsula: The Civil War Letters of General Philip Kearny*. Edited by William B. Styple, Kearny, NJ: Belle Grove Publishing, 1988.

Kelley, Dayton. *General Lee and Hood's Texas Brigade at the Battle of the Wilderness*. Hillsboro, TX: Hill Junior College Press, 1989.

King, Curtis S., William Glenn Robertson, and Steven E. Clay. *Staff Ride Handbook for the Overland Campaign, Virginia, 4 May to 15 June 1864: A Study in Operational-Level Command*. Fort Leavenworth, KS: Combat Studies Institute Press, 2006.

Krick, Robert K. "It Appeared As Though Mutual Extermination Would Put a Stop to the Awful Carnage." Edited by Gary W. Gallagher, *The Antietam Campaign*. Chapel Hill: The University of North Carolina Press, 1999, 222–58.

Kross, Gary. "Gettysburg Vignettes: Attack from the West, Vignette 1, Action on June 26." *Blue and Gray Magazine*, June 2000, 7–10.

La Fantasie, Glenn W. *Gettysburg Requiem: The Life and Lost Causes of Confederate Colonel William C. Oates*. Oxford: Oxford University Press, 2006.

Lee, Fitzhugh. Chancellorsville Address of General Fitzhugh Lee before the Virginia Division, A.N.V. Association, October 29, 1879. *Southern Historical Society Papers*. Vol. 7. Richmond, VA, December, 1879. Number 12.

Lee, Robert E. *The Wartime Papers of R. E. Lee*. Boston: Little, Brown, 1961.

Lincoln, Abraham. *The Collected Works of Abraham Lincoln.* Edited by Roy O. Basler. New Brunswick, NJ: Rutgers University Press, 1953–55.

Longacre, Edward G. *General Ulysses S. Grant: The Soldier and the Man,* Cambridge, MA: Da Capo Press, 2006.

Longacre, Edward G. *The Commanders of Chancellorsville.* Nashville, TN: Rutledge Hill Press, 2005.

Longstreet, James. *From Manassas to Appomattox.* Bloomington: Indiana University Press, 1960.

Longstreet, James. "The Campaign of Gettysburg," *Philadelphia Weekly Times,* November 3, 1877.

Loughborough, Mary A. *My cave life in Vicksburg. With letters of trial and travel. By a Lady.* New York: D. Appleton and Company, 1864.

Marshall, Charles. "Events Leading Up to the Battle of Gettysburg," *Southern Historical Society Paper,* Vol. 23, 1895, 205–29.

Marvel, William. "The Making of a Myth: Ambrose E. Burnside and the Union High Command at Fredericksburg," in *The Fredericksburg Campaign.* Edited by Gary W. Gallagher. Chapel Hill: The University of North Carolina Press, 1995, 1–25.

Marvel, William. "The Battle of Fredericksburg." *National Parks Civil War Series.* Fort Washington, PA: Eastern National Part and Monument Association, 1993.

McClure, Alexander K. *Colonel Alexander K. McClure's Recollections of Half a Century.* New York: AMS Press, 1976,

McFeely, William S. *Grant.* New York: W. W. North & Company, 1981.

McPherson, James M. *Crossroads of Freedom.* New York: Oxford University Press, 2001.

Meade, George G. *The Life and Letters of General George Gordon Meade.* 2 vols. New York: Scribner's, 1913.

Meade, George Gordon , editor. *Life and Letters of George Gordon Meade, Major General, United States Army.* New York: Charles Scribner's Sons, 1913.

Melcher, Brevet-Major Holman S. "An Experience in the Battle of the Wilderness," *War Papers Read Before the Commandery of the State of Maine, Military Order of the Loyal Legion of the United States.* 3 vols. Portland, ME: Military Order, 1898.

Mertz, Greg, Supervisory Historian, Fredericksburg and Spotsylvania National Military Park, email to author of June 19, 2006.

Mosby, John S. *The Memoirs of Colonel John S. Mosby.* Edited by Charles Welles Russell, 1917. Bloomington: Indiana University Press, 1959. New York: Barnes and Noble, 1985 and 2003. New York: AMS Press reprint, 1976.

Norton, Oliver W. *Strong Vincent and His Brigade at Gettysburg.* Chicago: [No Publisher Listed], 1909. Found in manuscript room, Library of Congress, Washington, DC.

Nosworthy, Brent. *The Bloody Crucible of Courage.* New York: Carroll & Graf, Publishers, 2003.

Oates, William C. *The war between the Union and the Confederacy, and its lost opportunities, with a history of the 15th Alabama regiment and the forty-eight battles in which it was engaged . . . the war between the United States and Spain.* New York: The Neale Publishing Company, 1905.

The Official Military Atlas of the Civil War (henceforth *Official Atlas*). By Major George B. Davis, U.S. Army; Leslie J. Perry, Civilian Expert; Joseph W. Kirkley, Civilian Expert; compiled by Capt. Calvin D. Cowles, 23rd U.S. Infantry Washington. D.C.: U.S. Government Printing Office, 1891–1895; Barnes and Noble Reprint Edition; Introduction by Richard Sommers, Ph.D., Archivist-Historian, U.S. Army Military History (Institute) New York: Barnes and Noble, 1985 and 2003

Olmstead, Frederick Law. *The Papers of Frederick Law Olmsted*, Vol. 4, *Defending the Union: The Civil War and the U.S. Sanitary Commission.* Edited by Jane Turner Censor. Baltimore, MD: Johns Hopkins University Press, 1986.

Perret, Geoffrey. *Lincoln's War.* New York: Random House, 2004.

Pfanz, Donald C. *Richard S. Ewell: A Soldier's Life.* Chapel Hill: University of North Carolina Press, 1998.

Pittman, Samuel E. *The Operations of General Alpheus S. Williams' Command in the Chancellorsville Campaign.* Detroit, MI: W. S. Ostler, Printer, 1888.

Pollard, Edward A. *Southern History of the War: The First Year of the War.* New York: Charles B. Richardson, 1864.

Pope, Major General, General Orders No. 19, August 14, 1862, text found http://www.civilwarhome.com/popesorders.htm

Porter, Horace. *Campaigning with Grant.* New York: The Century Company, 1897.

Powell, William H. *The Fifth Army Corps.* Dayton, OH: Morningside, 1984. Reprint of 1895 book.

Priest, John Michael. *Nowhere to Run: The Wilderness, May 4th & 5th, 1864.* Shippensburg, PA: White Mane Publishing, 1995.

Priest, John Michael. *Victory Without Triumph: The Wilderness, May 6th & 7th, 1864.* Shippensburg, PA: White Mane Publishing, 1996.

Pullen, John *The Twentieth Maine.* Dayton, OH: Morningside Bookshop, 1984. Reprint of 1957 edition.

Putnam, Douglas Jr. "Reminiscences of the Battle of Shiloh," *Sketches of War History, 1861–1865*, Military Order of the Loyal Legal of the United States, Ohio Commandery. Vol. 3, 197–211.

Rafuse, Ethan S. *McClellan's War: The Failure of Moderation in the Struggle for the Union.* Bloomington: Indiana University Press, 2005.

Rhea, Gordon C. *The Battle of the Wilderness.* Baton Rouge: Louisiana State University Press, 1994.

Richardson, Albert D. *A Personal History of Ulysses S. Grant.* Hartford, CT: American Publishing Company, 1868.

Robertson, James I., Jr. *Stonewall Jackson: The Man, The Soldier, The Legend.* New York: Macmillan Publishing, 1997.

Ropes, John Codman. *The Army under Pope.* New York: C. Scribner's Sons, 1885.

Rowland, Thomas J. *George B. McClellan and Civil War History: In the Shadow of Grant and Sherman.* Kent, OH: Kent State University Press, 1998.

Sandburg, Carl. *Abraham Lincoln: The War Years.* New York: Harcourt, Brace & Company, 1939.

Scott, Robert Garth. *Into the Wilderness with the Army of the Potomac.* Bloomington: Indiana University Press, 1983.

Sears, Stephen W. *Chancellorsville.* Boston: Houghton Mifflin Company, 1996.

Sears, Stephen W. *To the Gates of Richmond: The Peninsula Campaign.* New York: Ticknor & Fields, 1992.

Sears, Stephen W., editor. *The Civil War Papers of George B. McClellan: Selected Correspondence, 1861–1865.* New York: Ticknor & Fields, 1989.

Sears, Stephen W. *George B. McClellan: The Young Napoleon.* New York: Ticknor & Fields, 1988.

Sears, Stephen W. *Landscape Turned Red: The Battle of Antietam.* New Haven, CT: Ticknor and Fields, 1983.

Silbey, Joel, H. *A Respectable Minority: The Democratic Party in the Civil War Era, 1860–1868.* New York: Norton, 1977.

Simpson, Brooks D. "Great Expectations," in Gary W. Gallagher, editor, *The Wilderness Campaign.* Chapel Hill: The University of North Carolina Press, 1997, 1–35.

Simpson, Harold B. *Hood's Texas Brigade: Lee's Grenadier Guard.* Waco, TX: Texian Press, 1970.

Simpson Harold B. *Hood's Texas Brigade: Lee's Grenadier Guard.* Waco, TX: Texian Press, 1970.

Smalley, George N. *New York 'Tribune'* Narrative, September 17, 1862. Reprinted in Frank Moore, editor, Rebellion Record. New York: Arno Press reprint, 1977. Vol. 5, 466–72.

Smith, Derek. *Lee's Last Stand.* Shippensburg, PA: White Mane Books, 2002.

Smith, Gustavus W. *Confederate War Papers.* New York: Atlantic Publishing, 1884.

Smith, James Power. *Stonewall Jackson and Chancellorsville.* Richmond: R. E. Lee Camp No 1, Confederate Veterans, 1904.

Smith, Jean Edward. *Grant.* New York: Simon & Schuster, 2001.

Stackpole, Edward J. *From Cedar Mountain to Antietam.* Harrisburg, PA: The Stackpole Company, 1959.

Stewart, George R. *Pickett's Charge.* Boston: Houghton Mifflin Company, 1959.

Stoddard, William O. *Inside the White House in War Times.* New York: C. L. Webster and Co. 1880.

Sutherland, Daniel K. *Fredericksburg and Chancellorsville: The Dare Mark Campaign.* Lincoln: University of Nebraska Press, 1998.

Symonds, Craig L., The Confederate Military Effort in the West. Historical Text Archive © 2003 http://www.historicaltextarchive.com/sections.php?op=viewarticle&artid=660

Taafe, Stephen R. *Commanding the Army of the Potomac.* Lawrence: The University of Kansas Press, 2006.

Taylor, Walter H. *Four Years with General Lee.* Edited by James Robertson. New York: Bonanza Books, 1962.

Trudeau, Noah Andre. *Gettysburg: A Testing of Courage.* New York: Perennial, 2002.

Trudeau, Noah Andre. "The Walls of 1864," in Robert Crowley, editor, *With My Face to the Enemy: Perspectives on the Civil War.* New York: G. P. Putnam's Sons, 2001, 413–28.

Trudeau, Noah Andre. *The Last Citadel,* Boston: Little, Brown and Company, 1991.

Tsouras, Peter G., editor. *The Greenhill Dictionary of Military Quotations.* Mechanicsburg, PA: Stackpole Books, 2000.

U.S. Government, Department of Homeland Security, Office of Immigration Statistics, "Table 1: Immigration to the United States; Fiscal Years 1820–2004," *2004 Yearbook of Immigration Statistics,* January 2006.

U.S. Government, War Department, *Official Records of the War of the Rebellion.* Washington, D.C.: Government Printing Office, 1880–1900. Hard copy and "The Civil War CD ROM," published by Guild Press of America, 1997, 1998, 1999, 2000.

Van Doren, Carl. *The Literary Works of Abraham Lincoln.* Selected, with an Introduction, by Carl Van Doren. New York: The Heritage Press, 1942.

The Washington Times. "Crossroads: Vital Link in American History," *The Washington Times,* May 12, 2001.

The Washington Times. "Grant Inspires His Troops," *The Washington Times,* May 6, 2000.

Webb, Alexander S. "Through the Wilderness," in Robert Underwood Johnson and Clarence Buel, editors, *Battles and Leaders of the Civil War: The Way to Appomattox,* Vol. 4. New York: Castle Books Reprint 1956, 152–69.

Weigley, Russell. *A Great Civil War.* Bloomington: Indiana University Press, 2000.

Weld, Stephen Minot. *War Diary and Papers of Stephen Minot Weld.* Cambridge, MA: Riverside Press, 1979.

Wert, Jeffry D. *The Sword of Lincoln.* New York: Simon & Schuster. 2005.

Wilcox, Charles E. "With Grant at Vicksburg," Edgar L. Erickson, editor, *Journal of the Illinois State Historical Society.* Vol. 30, Number. 4, January 1938, 467.

Wiley, Bell I. *Road to Appomattox.* Memphis, TN: Memphis State College Press, 1956.

Wilkeson, Frank. *Recollections of a Private Soldier in the Army of the Potomac.* New York: G. P. Putnam's Sons, 1887.

Williams, A. M. *Sam Houston and the War of Independence.* Boston: Houghton Mifflin Co., 1893.

Williams, General Alpheus S. *From the Cannon's Mouth: The Civil War Letters of General Alpheus S. Williams,* edited with an introduction by Milo M. Quaife. Detroit, MI: Wayne State University Press, 1959.

Wilson, James Harrison. *Under the old flag; recollections of military operations in the War for the Union, the Spanish War, the Boxer Rebellion, etc.* Westwood, CT: Greenwood Press, 1971.

Worsham, John M. *One of Jackson's Foot Cavalry.* New York: The Neale Publishing Company, 1912.

INDEX

ABOUT THE AUTHOR

Bruce L. Brager, a graduate of George Washington University, is a writer who has ghostwritten dozens of books and published numerous titles under his own name, including *There He Stands: The Story of Stonewall Jackson*, *Petersburg*, and *Monitor vs. Merrimack*. He lives in New York City.